nF419132

Design by Greg Traverso
Photos by Ashley Shult Langdon

First edition, First printing 2024
First published in the United States in 2024

ISBN: 979-8-2181-9656-1 (paperback)
ISBN: 979-8-2181-9661-5 (ebook)

Printed in the United States by Ingram
Distributed in the United States and Worldwide by Ingram

Printed on FSC© certified materials.

Published by Mildly Scenic

MILDLY SCENIC
Sacramento, California
www.mildlyscenic.com

Library of Congress Cataloging-in-Publication Data is on file
for this title at https:/lcnn.loc.gov/2024903495.

PUBLISHER'S NOTE: While every effort has been made
to assure the accuracy of the information contained in this
book, it is a natural space that is subject to the effects of the
natural environment and city projects. This book is intended
as a starting point from which to begin the exploration of the
American River Parkway, and there are more trails and access
points than I've been able to document in this book. Follow
current laws, exercise necessary precautions, and keep the
river clean and safe for all of us. The author assumes no
liability for accidents happening to, or injuries sustained by
readers who engage in the activities described in this book.

FOR MY KIDS, DYLAN AND RHYS

The adventure is better with you in tow

MILDLY SCENIC

A TRAIL GUIDE TO SACRAMENTO'S LOWER AMERICAN RIVER

BY ASHLEY SHULT LANGDON

DESIGN BY GREG TRAVERSO

CONTENTS

MY STORY

When the entire world shut down in March of 2020, I left my job to care for our boys, ages three and five. Because of the COVID-19 pandemic, their preschool had closed. Playgrounds were off-limits. Museums, friends, babysitters—all gone. When my eldest started climbing out of the windows and rummaging through the garage in search of power tools, I knew I had to find a wild space to explore, both for my sanity and their safety. Thus began my discovery of the Lower American River — this incredible urban river that runs right through Sacramento County.

My first instinct was to pick up a book of hikes to get us started. I grew up in a family of travelers and hikers. My bookshelf is full of guidebooks like the *Lonely Planet* series and *60 Hikes within 60 Miles of Sacramento*. The first step to any adventure—especially as a group leader or parent—is to buy the book and do some research. I found several books about the American River Parkway. While interesting and valuable, the information in those volumes was largely focused on the history, the wildlife, and navigating the (absolutely gorgeous) paved bike path. What about places to splash in the river or have a picnic? What about the network of dirt trails? Most of those trails listed in hiking books took Sacramentans far away from the urban area, requiring an entire day set aside. At their ages, my kids couldn't last more than about 20 minutes in the car before losing their minds. I needed wild space close to home.

For the first six months of the pandemic, I took the boys out in the mornings and was home for naptime. I logged 60 days on the river, keeping a journal of the places we'd discovered. For us, the four-hour adventure from 9am-1pm was just the right amount of time to get the wiggles out by tree climbing, swimming, or rock throwing, having a picnic lunch and then riding out the warmest part of the day with some downtime at home.

During those initial adventures, I fine-tuned exactly what we needed to bring with us so we'd have enough snacks and water, as well as some sand toys, binoculars, or fishing poles to keep things interesting for the boys. It all had to fit into a Camelbak to keep our hands free and our backs unburdened by a heavy load. I discovered that it was equally important to stash a change of clothes or "cozy pants" in the car so no one had to ride home sandy or wet!

In the beginning it was springtime, so we were looking for butterflies, and mucking around in rainboots. By summer, it was all about the swimming spots and shady river banks. One day we might find ourselves on the north bank of the river, and we'd look across the way and spot a stretch of river that looked fun; the next day, we'd be on the south bank. And so it went—repeating the adventures we loved best, and noting how the seasons and the river flow altered our experiences.

Being a runner, I also started exploring the trails on Saturdays without the kids. I'd park in the same spot I took the kids during the week and piece together the many trails that wind along the river and into the natural spaces of the American River Parkway. This became the second type of adventure I wanted to share: walks and runs under five miles.

Some of the loops in this book I owe to my husband's discovery as a gravel cyclist. Occasionally we'll cross paths with one another miles away from home and out on the trails—he on bike and me on foot. We'll share our new discoveries back at home, hunched over Google maps and our Strava apps and zooming in on the new trail we've discovered.

In the future, I'd like to add biking and paddling adventures, but for now, this book will outline our favorite short adventures on foot—almost 70 of them.

Enjoy!

A QUIET MORNING ON THE RIVER

INTRODUCTION

There are many ways to explore the Lower American River and the green belt surrounding it, (also known as the American River Parkway). One could access the river from the same spot ten times and have a new adventure each time depending on the river flow, the season, the time of day, and who you've brought along with you. This book is perfect for bite-sized adventures: morning trail runs and half-day hikes under five miles, as well as picnic and swim spots within a half-mile from the car.

WHAT MAKES THE LOWER AMERICAN RIVER UNIQUE

The Lower American River, starting below the Nimbus Dam (at Hazel Ave.) and flowing down to its confluence with the Sacramento River (at Discovery Park), is the only urban waterway to be federally-designated as a Wild & Scenic River. And with good reason—the river provides the critical habitat and breeding grounds for the steelhead trout and the Chinook salmon, both of which are endangered species. In addition to the rich biological diversity found along the parkway, the Lower American River is the second-largest tributary to the Sacramento River, which feeds into the Delta providing water for drinking and farming for over half of the state of California. Recreationally, it is home to the American River Bike Trail, and provides a wilderness escape that runs right through metropolitan Sacramento.

I've divided the river into eighteen chapters, each one describing a distinct access point from which to begin a bite-sized adventure. The chapters begin at the bottom of the river in downtown Sacramento and end at Folsom Lake. Additional access points may be referenced within a chapter, and some are not mentioned in this book at all. This guide is intended as a starting point to piece together your own adventures.

Within each chapter, there are two kinds of bite-sized adventures: the close picnic spot about a half-mile from the car, and the longer 3-5 mile loop for the runners and walkers. A chart and a map provides the following details: ideal river-flow, sun exposure, beach type, trail type, activities, whether the area is dog-friendly, and parking.

SEASONS

Unlike some areas of California, Sacramento has four distinct seasons—and the river expresses each of them differently. Winter is damp, cool, green, and muddy, with salmon hopping upriver to spawn. In spring, the riverbanks explode into carpets of wildflowers, rushing rivers, goslings galore, butterflies, cool mornings, and warm afternoons. Summer is toasty and warm, which makes the river a perfect spot midday to swim, or early morning to run and then hop in the river in your running clothes to cool down. Fall colors can include vibrant reds and oranges, and the lowlight creates more opportunities for shady afternoon runs. The sunny stretches are to be avoided on a summer afternoon, but sought after on a frosty morning.

As you move upriver, you will notice the vegetation shifts from grasses and grape vines downriver, to oak trees and sugar pines up by the lakes. Coyotes, deer, otters, blue herons, egrets, bald eagles, geese, crawfish, and turtles are among the wildlife that can be seen. You may even spot some sea lions that have migrated from the Bay Area! The river is also home to over 40 species of fish, including the endangered steelhead trout and Chinook salmon.

While this book is not a field guide to the wildlife along the Lower American River, I have listed a few of the flora and fauna in the margins of each chapter to call attention to the shifting habitats as you move up river.

THE LANDSCAPE AND HUMAN INTERFERENCE

The landscape of the river is closely entwined with its history. In the 19th century, settlers took over the scenic valley from the indigenous Nisenan people. Gold mining and its destructive practices soon upturned the gravel bars and blasted away river banks, drastically altering the landscape. By the mid-1900s, the United States Bureau of Reclamation began taking steps to control the flow of the river; these included the construction of the Nimbus and Folsom dams, as well as the levees.

As the region's population grows and the climate warms, a coalition of federal authorities, resource managers, and conservationists are working to control river flow and restore wildlife habitat. There are two notable projects that have recently brought giant excavators to move rock and rubble in and around the river. The first of these is the Lower American River Erosion Protection

Construction. This project broke ground in the Spring of 2022, erasing many of the trails that wound around the riverbanks between Paradise Beach (Chapter 3) and the Guy West Bridge (Chapter 4). These efforts focus on protecting the River Park community by strengthening the levee that wraps around the neighborhood. The second project is the restoration of habitat vital to the salmon and steelhead trout that spawn in the gravel beds of the Lower American River. Most of the activity is found around Ancil Hoffman (Chapter 11) and Sailor Bar (Chapter 17).

TRAILS

Many of the trails in this book are referred to as "social trails," formed spontaneously by humans and animals navigating the riverbanks. Some trails have been used by fisherman for decades, while others date back to the days of the Pony Express in the mid 19th century. But this doesn't mean that, once established, these trails never change. Occasionally washed over by heavy rains or re-landscaped by city-wide projects, it is possible some of the trails I'm writing about will look different a few years from now.

There is one continuous multi-use trail that is maintained by American River Parkway Foundation volunteers and in many cases there are clear markers for hiking and equestrian use. Yellow posts are painted to identify trail entry points. In some areas, there is clearly one wide path that is the favorite. In other areas, there may be several trails that branch off from one another along the river. Most are sandwiched nicely between the American River Bike Trail and the river. When in doubt, stay close to the river to create any out-and-back adventure of your choice without getting turned around. Pay attention to the direction of river-flow and you'll know if you are headed down-river or upriver from your parked car.

A satellite map app on your phone is a handy way to see the fire roads and trails when you need the blue dot on the map to give you confidence. Most of the trails are interconnected and can be combined to create longer routes. Although this book documents many miles of trail, it is not comprehensive. Go forth and continue exploring!

WHAT TO PACK

Unless you're out for a run, you may want to bring along a few items to make your half-day adventure more enjoyable. I like to keep my hands free, so a backpack or hydration pack with extra clips to add on a few hats, plastic pail, or a rolled-up towel is handy.

EVERYDAY ADVENTURING:
  Backpack or hydration pack
  Sunscreen
  Snacks

EVERYDAY ADVENTURING WITH KIDS:
  Poop bags
  A few toys (e.g., shovel, truck, bug catcher, binoculars, wand) *
  Fishing poles

WARM WEATHER OPTIONAL ITEMS:
  Sun shirt
  Hat
  Goggles
  Towel or blanket
  Small pack chair
  Wagon
  Water shoes
  Life jacket
  Change of clothes (left in the car)

When the river is high, most of the beach spots are covered, while most trails remain.

Low: 2,500 CFS
High: 18,000+ CFS

MAP LEGEND

Here is a list of icons to help you navigate this book.

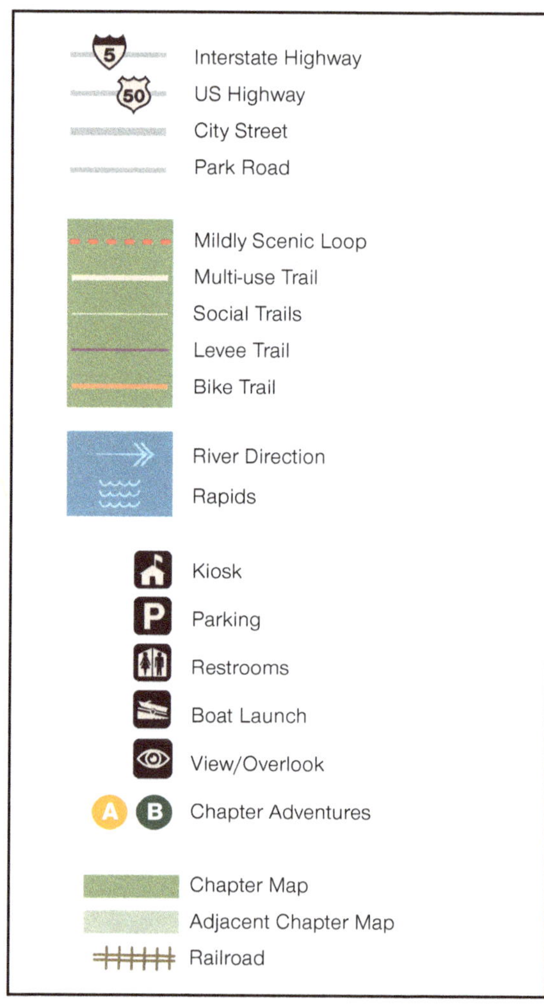

Trash – Although some access points have trash cans, many do not. Keep the area beautiful, clean, and safe by packing out any trash you create during your visit. Bonus points for bringing your own trash grabber and packing out a plastic bag of trash.

WHEN NATURE CALLS

It is inevitable, especially when adventuring with kids, that you'll find yourself uncomfortably far from the bathroom at the parking lot. Bring a poop bag, such as the ones dog owners carry, and pack it out. Alternatively, you can use the sand toys to dig a hole six inches deep. Always pack out the toilet paper.

PERSONAL SAFETY

Exercise caution when enjoying the wilderness. The Lower American is an urban river, which brings the joy of accessibility for all of us city dwellers. You will likely encounter others during your visit. Families, college students, people living in tents and everyone in between enjoy the river for its solitude and beauty. Downriver from Watt Ave and closer to the grid, it is more common to find tents tucked in the brush. Most people living away from urban streets would like to avoid you just as much as you'd like to avoid them. If you are nervous about encountering a stranger during your adventures, bring along a friend or a pet.

HYDRATION

Be mindful of dehydration, especially during the warm months. Unless it is winter, plan your adventure for the morning hours and know that by mid-afternoon the sun will be relentless and the walk back to the car may be extremely hot. Bring lots of water, a big hat, a sunshade, and sunscreen if you plan to be out on a summer afternoon.

SWIMMING

Know your limits and the abilities of those swimming with you. Much of the river is shallow and slow-moving. Depending on the season or the river flow, however, the current can be swift and the river deep. Put the small ones in life jackets—many access points even have free ones to loan as part of the "Life Looks Good on You" initiative. Where possible, I've given a recommendation for ideal river flow.

You can check the river flow at: cdec.water.ca.gov/river

You can check river temperature at: www.waterforum.org

RATTLESNAKES

Watch for rattle snakes sunning themselves on the trails, and be mindful when exploring off trails.

POISON OAK

Depending on the season, this three-leafed plant can be red or green.

PARKING Most access points between Discovery Park and Sailor Bar are operated by Sacramento County Parks & Recreation and cost $7 per vehicle. The parking fee can be paid at the kiosks upon entry. Alternatively, a Regional Parks Annual Park Pass is $70 ($35 for seniors over age 65) and can be purchased through www.sacparks.net.

California State Parks operates and manages the area around Lake Natoma. Kiosks are generally staffed by state park rangers, who will sell either a daily parking pass ($10), or an annual pass ($125). Passes can be borrowed from your local public library.

You can also access the river trails via the neighborhoods without paying a fee. In many of the chapters, these alternative parking options are listed. Be respectful when parking on neighborhood streets so as to keep these access points open to the public.

ACCESS POINTS

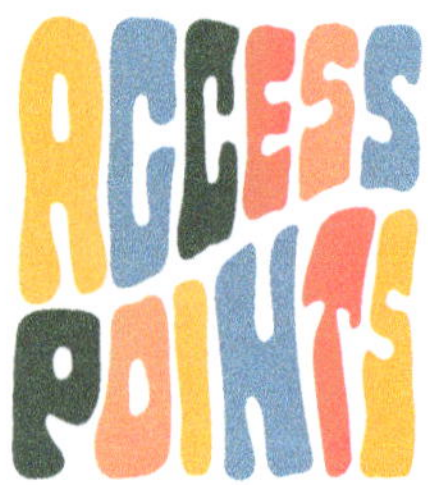

1
DISCOVERY PARK

2
SUTTERS LANDING

3
PARADISE BEACH

4
GUY WEST BRIDGE

5
WATT AVE RIVER ACCESS

6
GRISTMILL RECREATION AREA

7
ESTATES DR. TO JACOB LN.

8
WILLIAM B POND

9
SARAH COURT

10
RIVER BEND PARK

11
ANCIL HOFFMAN

12
HAGAN COMMUNITY PARK

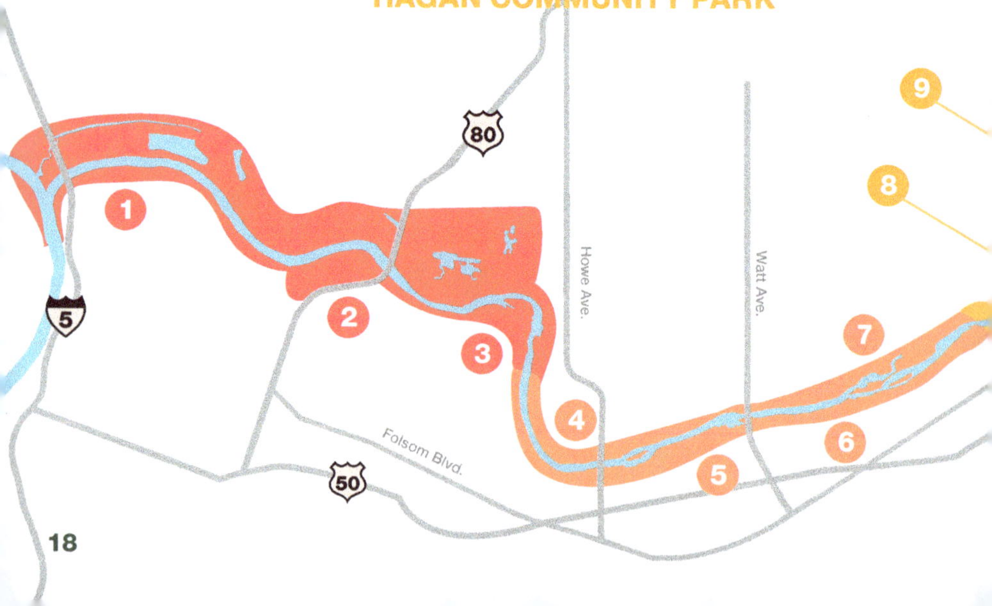

13
ROSSMOOR BAR
14
EL MANTO
15
SUNRISE RECREATION AREA
16
BANNISTER PARK
17
SAILOR BAR
18
LAKE NATOMA
Sunrise Blvd.
Folsom Blvd.
50
11
16
17
15
13
14
12
10
18

TRAILS AT A GLANCE

	PARKING	TYPE	DISTANCE	RIVER		EXPOSURE	
				LOW RIVER	HIGH RIVER	SUN	SHADE
1. DISCOVERY PARK	$6						
A. Tiscornia Park Beach		Picnic	0.1	●	●	●	●
B. Walk to Old Sacramento		Run	1.0	●	●	●	
2. SUTTERS LANDING	$7						
A. Main Beach		Picnic	0.1	●		●	●
B. Upriver Loop		Run	3.5	●	●	●	●
3. PARADISE BEACH	FREE						
A. Main Beach		Picnic	0.1	●		●	
B. Backside Beach		Picnic	0.5	●		●	●
C. Downriver Loop		Run	3.5	●	●	●	●
D. Upriver Bridge Loop		Run	4.0	●	●	●	
4. GUY WEST BRIDGE	FREE						
A. Bridge Loop		Run	5.5	●	●	●	●
5. WATT AVENUE	$7						
A. Boat Launch Beach		Picnic	0.1	●	●		●
B. Downriver Spot		Picnic	0.2	●		●	
C. Rocky Wash		Picnic	0.2	●		●	
D. Loop to Gristmill		Run	4.5	●	●	●	●
6. GRISTMILL RECREATION AREA	$7						
A. Rocky Beach		Picnic	0.3	●		●	
B. Shell Beach		Picnic	1.0	●		●	
C. Loop to Waterton Way River Access		Run	3.0	●	●	●	
7. ESTATES DRIVE TO JACOB LANE	FREE						
A. River Spot at Ashton Drive		Picnic	0.1	●		●	
B. River Spot Among the Reeds		Picnic	0.5	●	●		●
C. River Spot to the Peninsula		Picnic	1.2	●		●	
D. Loop to Harrington River Access		Run	3.0	●	●	●	●
8. WILLIAM B POND	$7						
A. Clay Banks		Picnic	0.1	●	●	●	
B. Beach Downriver		Picnic	0.5	●		●	
C. Small Hike to the Wash		Walk	2.0	●	●	●	●
D. Arden Pond		Walk	0.1	●	●	●	
E. Loop Upriver (to Hagan Park)		Run	6.0	●	●	●	●
F. Loop Downriver (to Ashton Drive)		Run	6.0	●	●	●	●
9. SARAH COURT	FREE						
A. Clay Banks		Picnic	0.1	●		●	
B. Sandy Point		Picnic	0.3	●		●	
10. RIVER BEND PARK	$7						
A. River Spot at Lower Parking Lot		Picnic	0.1	●	●	●	
B. River Spot at Upper Parking lot		Picnic	0.1	●	●	●	
C. River Spot at Cordova Creek		Run	1.0	●		●	
D. Loop Around River Bend Park		Run	3.0	●	●	●	●

BEACH TYPE			TRAIL TYPE			ACTIVITIES				COMPANIONS			
SAND	ROCKS	CLAY	DIRT	LEVEE/GRAVEL	BIKE PATH	RUNNING	PICNIC	WADING	SWIMMING	BOAT LAUNCH	DOGS	KIDS	ACCESSIBLE
●							●	●		●	●	●	●
				●		●					●		●
●							●	●	●		●	●	●
			●	●	●	●					●		
●			●				●	●	●		●	●	●
●			●				●	●	●		●	●	
			●	●		●					●		
			●	●	●	●					●		●
			●	●	●	●							●
●		●						●		●	●	●	●
●			●				●	●	●		●	●	
	●		●				●	●			●	●	
			●	●	●	●					●		
	●			●	●					●	●	●	
		●					●	●	●			●	●
			●			●					●	●	
		●	●				●	●	●		●	●	
●			●			●	●	●	●		●	●	
	●		●				●	●	●		●	●	
			●	●	●	●					●	●	
		●	●				●	●	●		●	●	●
●			●				●	●	●		●	●	
	●		●				●	●	●		●	●	●
		●	●				●	●	●		●	●	
			●		●	●					●	●	
			●	●	●	●					●	●	
		●					●	●			●	●	●
●			●				●	●	●		●	●	
	●						●	●	●	●	●	●	
	●						●	●	●		●	●	
		●	●				●	●			●	●	
			●			●					●		

TRAILS AT A GLANCE

	PARKING	TYPE	DISTANCE	RIVER		EXPOSURE	
				LOW RIVER	HIGH RIVER	SUN	SHADE
11. ANCIL HOFFMAN	**$7**						
A. Effie Yeaw Rocky Wash		Picnic	1.0	●	●	●	●
B. Climbing Tree/Dinosaur Nest		Picnic	0.1	●	●	●	●
C. Beach Spot with Small Shady Trees		Picnic	0.1	●	●	●	●
D. Loop Around Golf Course		Run	3.0	●	●		●
E. Loop Around Effie Yeaw Trails		Run	2.0	●	●		●
12. HAGAN COMMUNITY PARK	**FREE**						
A. Water Tower Banks		Picnic	0.1	●		●	
B. Gilligan's Islands		Picnic	1.0	●		●	
C. Loop Upriver to Rossmoor Bar		Run	3.5	●	●	●	●
13. ROSSMOOR BAR	**$7**						
A. Beach Near Parking Lot		Picnic	0.1	●	●	●	
B. Beach Upriver		Picnic	0.5	●	●	●	
C. Loop Around Rossmoor Bar		Run	2.2	●	●	●	
14. EL MANTO	**$7**						
A. Clay Banks		Picnic	0.5	●	●	●	
B. San Juan Rapids Downriver		Picnic	0.5	●		●	
C. Loop to Lower Sunrise		Run	4.0	●	●	●	●
15. SUNRISE RECREATION AREA	**$7**						
A. River Spot Below Bridge		Picnic	0.1	●			●
B. Salmon Spotting		Picnic	0.1	●	●	●	
C. Loop Upriver to Nimbus Hatchery		Run	3.5	●	●	●	●
D. Loop Downriver to El Manto		Run	4.0	●	●		●
16. BANNISTER PARK	**FREE**						
A. River Spot at San Juan Rapids		Picnic	1.0	●		●	
B. River Spot Downriver from the Bridge		Picnic	1.0	●		●	
C. Loop around Bannister Park		Run	3.0	●	●	●	
17. SAILOR BAR	**$7**						
A. Grassy Bluff		Picnic	0.1	●	●	●	
B. Beach Spot		Picnic	1.0	●	●		●
C. Shallow Beach		Picnic	0.5	●		●	
D. Salmon Spotting		Picnic	0.1	●		●	●
E. Loop Around Sailor Bar		Run	3.5	●	●	●	●
18. LAKE NATOMA							
A. Nimbus Flat	$10	Any	2-4	●	●	●	
B. Willow Creek	$10	Any	2-4	●	●	●	
C. Black Miners Bar	$10	Any	2-4	●	●	●	●
D. Snipes-Pershig Ravine	FREE	Any	1.5		●		●
E. Mississippi Bar	FREE	Any	6.0	●		●	

BEACH TYPE			TRAIL TYPE			ACTIIVITIES				COMPANIONS			
SAND	ROCKS	CLAY	DIRT	LEVEE/GRAVEL	BIKE PATH	RUNNING	PICNIC	WADING	SWIMMING	BOAT LAUNCH	DOGS	KIDS	ACCESSIBLE
	•		•			•	•	•			•	•	•
	•						•	•	•		•	•	
•		•					•	•	•		•	•	
			•		•	•						•	•
			•									•	•
		•					•	•			•	•	
		•	•			•	•	•	•		•	•	
			•		•	•					•	•	
•							•	•	•	•	•	•	
•						•	•	•	•		•	•	
			•			•					•	•	
		•					•	•	•		•	•	
	•		•	•		•	•	•	•		•	•	
			•		•	•					•	•	
		•					•	•	•	•	•	•	•
		•					•	•	•		•	•	•
			•			•					•	•	
			•		•	•					•	•	
	•			•		•	•	•	•		•	•	
	•		•		•	•	•	•	•		•	•	
			•	•	•	•					•	•	
		•					•	•			•	•	•
	•		•			•	•	•	•		•	•	
	•		•	•		•	•	•	•		•	•	
	•	•	•					•		•		•	
			•			•					•	•	
•			•		•	•	•	•	•	•		•	•
			•		•	•	•	•	•		•	•	•
•		•	•		•	•	•	•	•	•	•	•	•
	•		•	•		•	•	•	•		•	•	
			•	•	•	•	•	•	•		•	•	

1
DISCOVERY PARK

195 Jibboom St., Sacramento, CA 95811

THE SAND IS SOFT UNDER THE JIBBOOM ST. BRIDGE

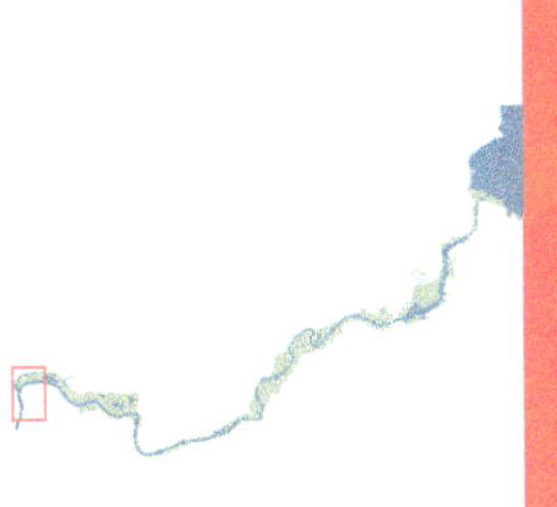

OVERVIEW

Located at the confluence of the Sacramento and the American rivers, Discovery Park is visible from Hwy. 50, just one mile from the quaint tourist destination of Old Town Sacramento. Because of its proximity to downtown, it is a popular destination on warm weekends. Boaters can launch their watercraft and head up either river from here.

For a river experience, enter through the south entrance, also called Tiscornia Park. The deep sand on this beach will please the sandcastle engineer in your family. For an urban feel, cozy up underneath Jibboom St. Bridge to enjoy the shade. Avoid swimming, as the E.coli levels are reportedly high here.

The Northgate entrance is accessible via the Garden Highway and leads to a grassy park that includes a boat launch, an archery field, restrooms, and picnic tables.

GETTING THERE

Take I-5 to the Richards Blvd. exit West. Turn right onto Jibboom St. and stay left to park before crossing the Jibboom St. Bridge. Parking $7, or Parks Annual Pass.

AMENITIES

Bathrooms, picnic tables, boat launch, archery, equestrian staging.

IDEAL RIVER-FLOW:
Any

SUN EXPOSURE:
Full sun/shade

BEACH TYPE:
Sand

TRAIL TYPE:
Dirt trails, bike path

ACTIVITIES:
Kids, picnics, wading, running, walking

DOG-FRIENDLY:
Yes

PARKING:
$7

LOOK FOR:
Cottonwood tree
Blackberry
California wild grape

Jiboom St. Bridge
P
A
B
Richards Blvd.
Jiboom St.
5
SACRAMENTO RIVER
SACRAMENTO
WEST SACRAMENTO
I Street Bridge
OLD SACRAMENTO
I Street

BONUS ADVENTURE

Put your dancing shoes on because Discovery Park is the backdrop for several music festivals throughout the year.

A TISCORNIA PARK BEACH

0.1 mile, Sun/partial shade, Swimming, Wading, Sand

Park at the far end of Tiscornia Park and find some shade by the edge of the confluence. The water is good for wading at the river's edge, but becomes deep in some areas—stay mindful of the current if wading. As mentioned above, the water quality is not recommended for swimming.

VARIATION: *Park closer to the bridge and walk down the bluff. The shade from the Jibboom St. Bridge, combined with the deep sand and mostly still, deep water makes it a great place for a picnic.*

B WALK TO OLD SACRAMENTO

1 mile, Sun, Walking, Running, Biking

If you pick up a book on urban walks or 'hikes' in Sacramento, the walk to Old Sacramento is probably included—but not because it's especially scenic. If you're downtown and already visiting Old Sacramento for the kitschy salt-water taffy, the Ferris wheel, or the (fantastic) California State Railroad Museum, then you might want to wander up the trail for some fresh air and river views. The Sacramento River is large and murky at this downtown location and there will be unsavory sights. Bring a friend.

SUTTERS LANDING

20 28th St., Sacramento, CA 95816

SUNSET OVER SUTTERS LANDING

OVERVIEW

If you live or work in downtown Sacramento Sutter's Landing offers a small slice of nature and glittery waters just a few blocks from the restaurants and bars. That said, as a result of its accessibility from midtown, there are often more encampments tucked off these trails than in some more remote locations. Motor boats can still make it up to this beach easily from downriver so you may end up in the middle of a boisterous boat-culture atmosphere. The sand is deep and fluffy around here, which makes it an enjoyable destination for dogs and children alike.

THE TWO RIVERS TRAIL

Currently under construction, this 2.4 mile multi-use path will stretch along the south bank of the American River from downtown to Sacramento State, eventually providing an alternative to the American Bike River Trail (which already runs along the north bank). As of the writing of this book, there is a half-mile paved section from the parking lot to the Union Pacific Railroad bridge.

GETTING THERE

From Hwy. 50, take Hwy. 80 north to the H St. exit west. Turn right on 28th St., driving up and over the train tracks. Park by the outdoor skate park. Walk down the levee to the river. No fee.

AMENITIES

Skate park, bocce ball court, paved bike path, dog park

IDEAL RIVER-FLOW:
Any

SUN EXPOSURE:
Full sun/shade

BEACH TYPE:
Sand

TRAIL TYPE:
Dirt trails, bike path

ACTIVITIES:
Kids, picnics, wading, running, walking

DOG-FRIENDLY:
Yes

PARKING:
No Fee

LOOK FOR:
Wood ducks
Willow
Walnut tree

A MAIN BEACH

0.1 mile, Sun/partial shade, Swimming, Wading, Sand

Park at the skate park and walk directly down the levee to the beach. There is plenty of beach upriver, so it may be worth a little stroll to get some sand for yourself. The riverbank is shallow and great for splashing with small kids. The middle of the river is deep and swift, so be mindful if you choose to swim.

B UPRIVER LOOP

3.5 mile, Shady trail, Running, Walking, Dogs

Park at the skate park and run upriver along the trail that winds along the bluffs at the river's edge, about 0.8 mile to the Union Pacific Railroad crossing overhead. The trail merges into a gravel road that runs underneath Hwy. 80 and up

to the levee behind River Park. Continue another 0.5 miles along the levee until you see a trail branch off to your left and down to the river. Stay on this scenic riverside trail another 0.5 mile until you reach the creek crossing, a good turnaround point to retrace your steps.

VARIATIONS: *Continue another 0.5 mile to reach Paradise Beach before turning around, taking the levee back to form a loop.*

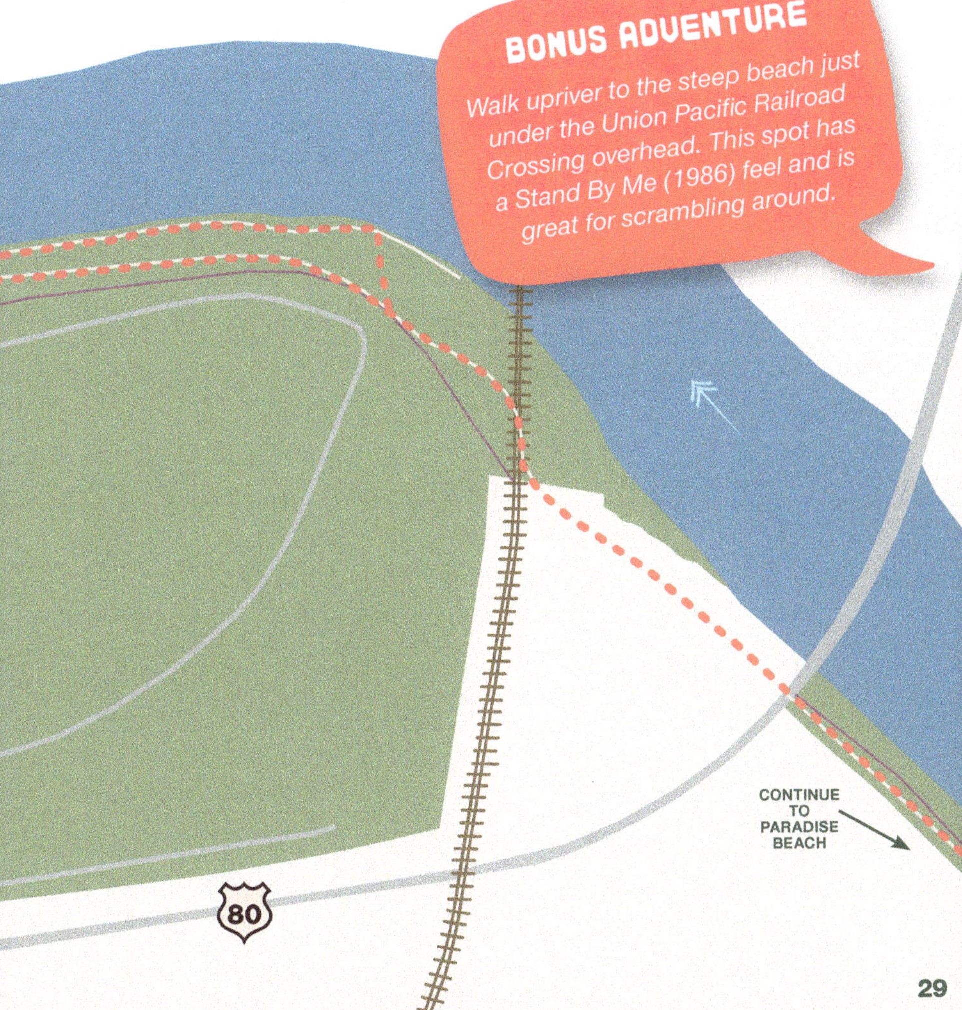

3

PARADISE BEACH

5415 Sandburg Dr., Sacramento, CA 95819

THE SHALLOW WATERS ARE GREAT FOR KIDS.

OVERVIEW

Paradise Beach has been a favorite spot since the late 1800s, and was the first piece of land purchased for the American River Parkway in the 1950s.

As you stand atop the levee, it may not be immediately clear why it is such a longstanding Sacramento favorite. The first few times I went to Paradise Beach, tucked in the River Park neighborhood, I wandered out toward the river and ended up on a mediocre pebbly beach that was too hot to drag my kids any farther. But after a little exploring, I was able to find what made this spot so special. If you follow this map, you'll quickly understand why it's called "paradise": the sand is deep and fluffy and the river runs slowly. In many places, you can wade shin-deep 30 yards out into the river. Dogs, children and bikers roam happily in this space.

GETTING THERE

From Hwy. 50, take Hwy. 80 North to the H St. exit East. Turn left Carlson Dr. until it ends at Glenn Hall Park. There is a large, free parking lot by the public pool.

AMENITIES

Glen Hall Park, adjacent to Paradise Beach, has flush toilets, soccer field, playground, tennis courts, public pool, and life jackets.

 MAIN BEACH

0.1 mile, Sun/partial shade, Swimming, Wading, Sand

At the bottom of the levee, take the trail that runs to your left and make your way to the river. Although short, the walk is wide open and sunny, so bring a hat. You'll find yourself on the top of a bluff looking down on an inlet perfect for swimming, wading, and balancing atop the big log that sits in the shallow water. Keep your eyes peeled for the occasional sea lion that comes up from the Bay Area in search of tasty fish!

Alternative spots downriver from here offer shade, as well as more sand bars—perfect for splashing or skin boarding.

B BACKSIDE BEACH

0.5 mile, Sun/partial shade, Swimming, Wading, Sand

If you're looking for a quieter spot, follow the main beach around the lagoon's edge and upriver. There's another tree for shade, a sandy river bank, and an island to wade onto and play pirates. If the river is high, the trail will be flooded.

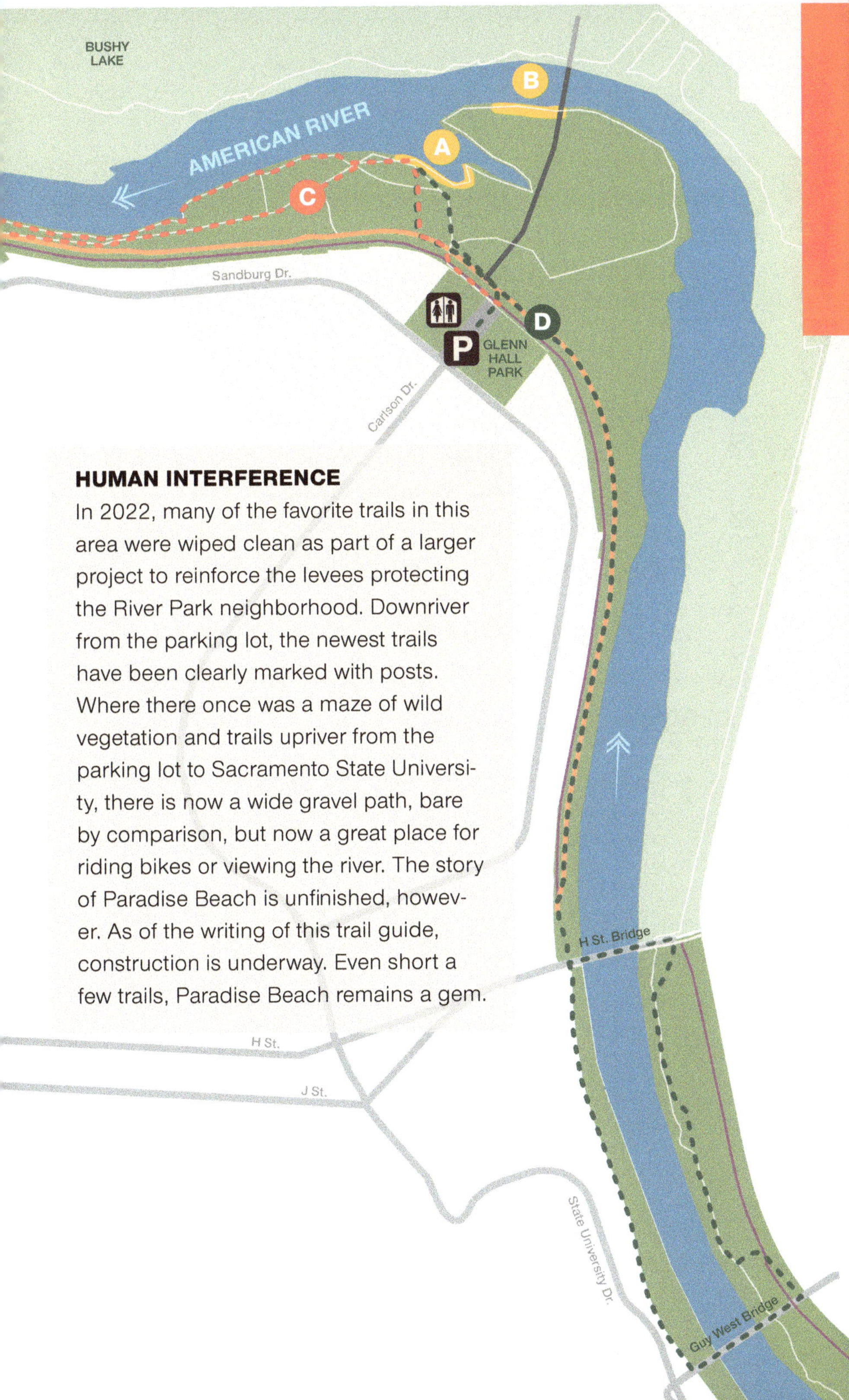

HUMAN INTERFERENCE

In 2022, many of the favorite trails in this area were wiped clean as part of a larger project to reinforce the levees protecting the River Park neighborhood. Downriver from the parking lot, the newest trails have been clearly marked with posts. Where there once was a maze of wild vegetation and trails upriver from the parking lot to Sacramento State University, there is now a wide gravel path, bare by comparison, but now a great place for riding bikes or viewing the river. The story of Paradise Beach is unfinished, however. As of the writing of this trail guide, construction is underway. Even short a few trails, Paradise Beach remains a gem.

C DOWNRIVER LOOP

3.5 mile, Sun/shade, Running, Walking, Dogs

From the parking lot, head up and over the levee and follow the trails to your left until you reachthe main beach. Head downriver along one of the several bluff trails. Where the beach ends, the trail continues along the water 1 mile along a trail. Some locals refer to as Beaver Trail, named for the active nocturnal residents. Before connecting to the levee, loop back along the dirt road below the levee to the parking lot. There is a wide, shady middle trail that is worth exploring once you get your bearings.

VARIATION: *Instead of looping back, continue under Hwy. 80 and all the way to Sutter's Landing (an additional 1.3 mile).*

D UPRIVER BRIDGE LOOP

4 mile, Sun/partial shade, Swimming, Sand, Running/Walking

Including a bridge in a run is always fun—and this trail has two! From the parking lot, run along the levee until you pass underneath the J St. Bridge. Continue along the top of the paved path until you reach the Guy West Bridge at Sacramento State. Cross this beautiful foot bridge and then run downriver on the north side of the river. I prefer to run along the bike path, but the trail underneath the levee is scenic as well. When you reach the J St. Bridge, cross back to the south side of the river and head back along the levee or the river trails.

VARIATIONS: *Stay on the levee the entire way, even along the north side.*

Make it a three-bridge run and continue all the way to Watt Ave. (5 miles more).

SPRING ARRIVES IN PARADISE

4

GUY WEST BRIDGE

997 University Ave., Sacramento, CA 95825

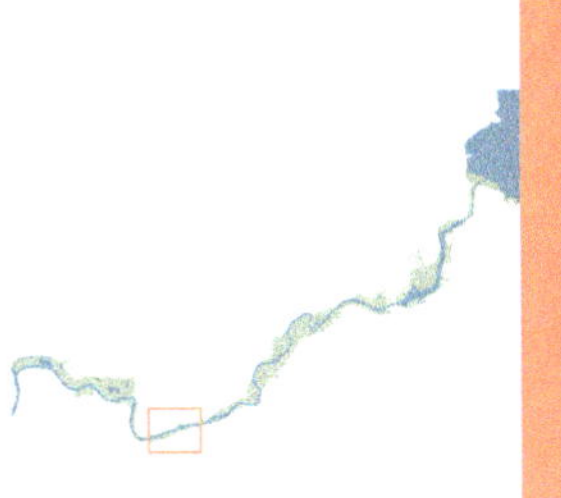

OVERVIEW

The Guy West Bridge is a destination in itself. Resembling a miniature Golden Gate Bridge, it is only for pedestrians and cyclists and it is a great way to access Sacramento State without having to navigate the campus itself. The bridge is scenic and offers a great place to take in the view. After a rainstorm, this is a great spot to watch the rushing river below.

There isn't a beach spot that I recommend from this access point, but there are many variations on foot both along the river as well as into Sacramento State that make it well worth the trip.

GETTING THERE

From Hwy. 50, take Howe Ave. and turn onto University Ave., which winds through the pocket neighborhood of Campus Commons. Park on the north side of the Guy West Bridge along University Ave. No fee.

ALTERNATIVE ACCESS POINTS

Sac State University Campus
Howe River Access
Watt Ave. River Access
University River Park Access
Kadema Dr. River Access
Glenbrook Park River Access

AMENITIES

Pit toilets, picnic tables, signs

Ⓐ BRIDGE LOOP

*5.5 miles, Partial shade,
Running, Walking*

This loop run will take you from the Guy West Bridge to the Watt Ave. Bridge, and back along the opposite side of the river.

The American River Bike Trail runs along the north bank of the river here, so there are more people, as well as a few bathrooms, park benches, and trail markers.

Along the south bank, the trail is also paved, but is less maintained. Between the river and the bike path, you will find multiple dirt trails to explore and plenty of shade to keep you cool. Under the Howe Ave. and Watt Ave. bridges, there may be more encampments tucked away, so be mindful. For an equally scenic loop, skip the trails and stick to the shoulder of the paved bike path.

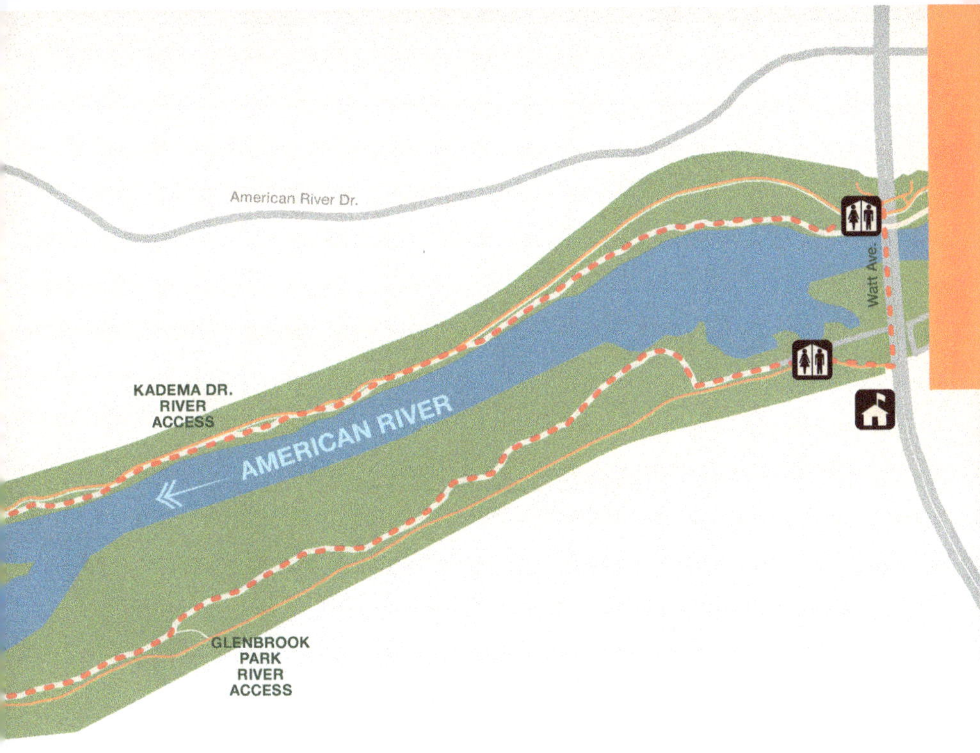

VARIATIONS: Remain on the north side of the river to Watt and continue as far as you like to William B Pond (4 miles more, one way).

Skip the less-populated south bank, and remain on the north bank of the river for an out-and-back

Bring a bike and follow this loop along the paved bike path.

BONUS ADVENTURE

Spend an afternoon exploring Sacramento State's picturesque campus, which has an arboretum and plenty of paved pathways winding through campus. This is a great place to scooter with kids. Also, the gingko trees near Mariposa Hall are absolutely stunning in the fall.

WATT AVENUE RIVER ACCESS

8703 La Riviera Dr., Sacramento, CA 95826

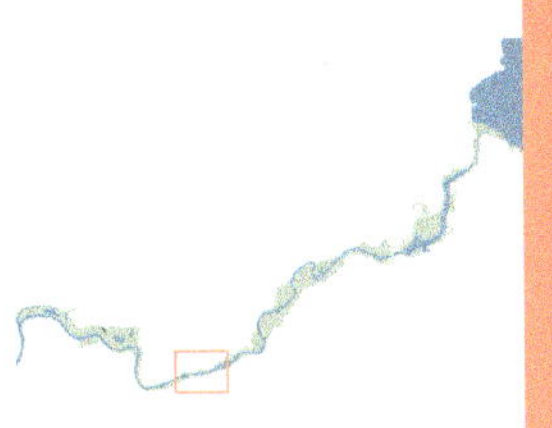

OVERVIEW

The Watt Ave. access point is located directly off of Hwy. 50. This makes the beach spots less pristine than elsewhere, and the noise of the traffic above along Watt Ave. bridge may detract from your enjoyment of an otherwise beautiful day. If you follow a trail toward the river, you might stumble upon some pizza boxes and an overnight shelter. That said, the wildlife is undeterred and thrives along these shores and in the marshy river habitat.

GETTING THERE

Take Hwy. 50 to Watt Ave. North exit, then turn onto La Riviera Dr. under the bridge. Parking $7, or Parks Annual Pass.

ALTERNATIVE ACCESS POINTS

Waterton Way River Access
SARA Park

AMENITIES

Bathrooms, water, boat launch, picnic tables, benches

IDEAL RIVER-FLOW:
Low to medium

SUN EXPOSURE:
Full sun/partial shade

BEACH TYPE:
Clay and sand

TRAIL TYPE:
Dirt trail, bike trail

ACTIVITIES:
Kids, picnics, swimming, wading, running, walking

DOG-FRIENDLY:
Yes - on leash

PARKING:
$7

LOOK FOR:
Valley oak tree
Gopher snake
Quail

HOT TIP

Park at one of the alternative access points for a quiet stretch of river.

A BOAT LAUNCH BEACH

0.0 mile, Sun/partial shade, Swimming, Wading, Rocks

For a simple access point or place to swim, park by the boat launch. The beach is located just upriver.

B DOWNRIVER SPOT

0.2 mile, Sun/partial shade, Swimming, Wading, Sand

For a little more privacy, walk downriver from the boat launch along the trail (about five minutes) until you see a small, sandy beach. If digging in the sand or building sandcastles is on your agenda, this will be a good spot.

C ROCKY WASH

0.2 mile, Sun/partial shade, Swimming, Wading, Rocks

A popular destination for fisherman, walk out along the gravel bar that extends just below the Watt Ave. Bridge.

D LOOP TO GRISTMILL

4.5 miles, Sun/partial shade, Running, Walking

Park at the farthest point upriver and follow the beautiful gravel trail, shaded by old oaks, to Gristmill Recreation Area. In the stretch between Watt Ave. and the creek crossing, there can be overnighters tucked in the bushes down along the river, where the water is marshy and stagnant. Stay on the wide and well-used wooded trail. At the foot bridge, the trail will split making a loop around the Gristmill Recreation Area.

VARIATIONS: *Park in the small neighborhood parking lot just upriver from Watt Ave., locate off La Riviera on Waterton Way, operated by SARA (Save the American River Association).*

HUMAN INTERFERENCE

As of the publishing of this book, the stretch of river bank east of Watt Ave has been identified as the U.S. Army Corps of Engineers (USACE) next "bank erosion" project.

If action is not taken, the trees and everything along the river bank will be bulldozed. Visit americanrivertrees.org to learn more.

6

GRISTMILL RECREATION AREA

9517 Mira Del Rio Dr., Sacramento, CA 95827

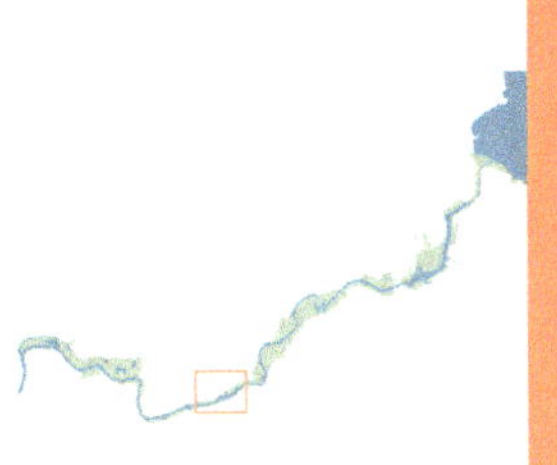

OVERVIEW

This quiet access point along the south bank of the river is located directly across from Harrington Way Access. Because of this, it is a great spot for launching boats and wandering the trails. Keep your eyes peeled for coyotes trotting along the paths. Go in the spring and enjoy the plethora of poppies!

The trails here are unpaved and extend in only one direction (downriver to Watt Ave.). At the top of this access point lies the Kassis Property, a rare 40-acres of riverfront open space that until recently was privately owned. On a clear day, the snow-capped Sierra Nevada are visible in the distance.

This access point derives its name from a gristmill owned by Swiss immigrant John Sutter. Sutter began construction on the mill in 1848 but never finished—his builders left mid-project to join the gold rush.

GETTING THERE

From Hwy. 50, exit Watt Ave. south, left on Folsom Blvd., left on Mira del Rio Dr., then left into the park. Follow the long paved road down to park by the boat launch. Parking $7/day, or Parks Annual Pass.

ALTERNATIVE ACCESS POINTS

Waterton Way River Access

SARA Park

AMENITIES

Bathrooms, benches and signs

IDEAL RIVER-FLOW:
Any

SUN EXPOSURE:
Full sun

BEACH TYPE:
Clay, pebbles, rocks

TRAIL TYPE:
Dirt and gravel

ACTIVITIES:
Kids, picnics, swimming, wading, running, walking

DOG-FRIENDLY:
Yes - on leash

PARKING:
$7

LOOK FOR:
Coyote
Great Horned Owl
Mistletoe

A   ROCKY BEACH

0.25 mile, Sun/partial shade, Swimming, Wading, Rocks

At the parking lot, walk down to the boat launch and out onto the very long, rocky wash that extends downriver. Great for skipping stones and feeling like an explorer on a remote island.

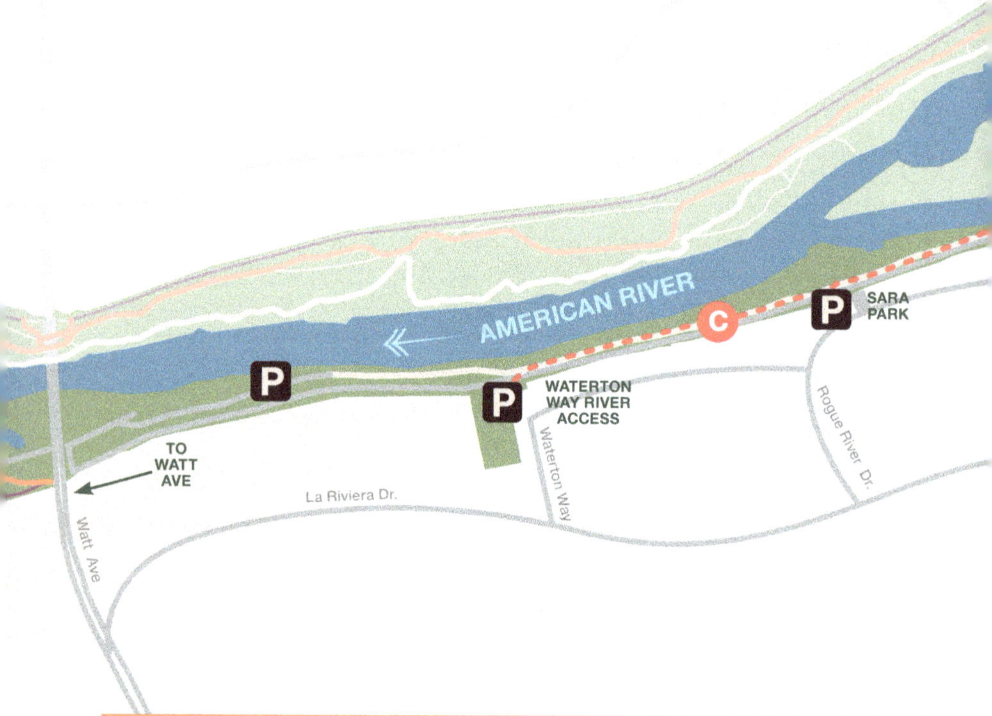

B   SHELL BEACH

1 mile, Sun/partial shade, Swimming, Wading, Sand

From the parking lot, walk downriver along the trail about a half-mile until you see a small sandy beach.

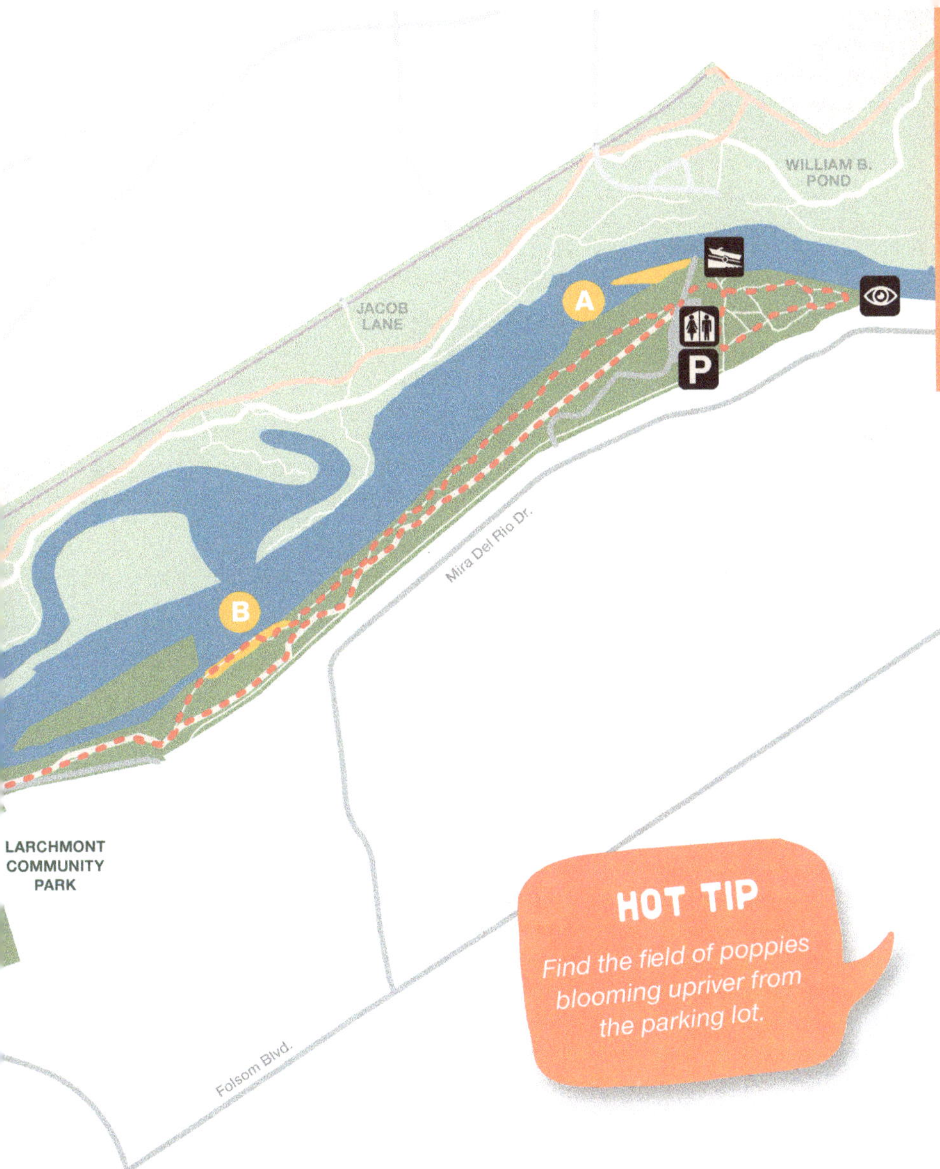

C LOOP TO WATERTON WAY RIVER ACCESS

4.5 miles, Sun/partial shade, Running, Walking

At the parking lot, follow the trail downriver along the bluff as it winds toward the footbridge of a city drainage creek and along the wooded trail. Continue past the bridge to Waterton Way or Watt Ave. Follow the inland trail back for variety.

VARIATIONS: *Add a half-mile loop upriver from the parking lot, and stop to stretch at the painted bench on the bluff.*

7

ESTATES DRIVE TO JACOB LANE

350 Estates Dr., Sacramento, CA 95864

VIEW FROM THE BOTTOM OF JACOB LANE

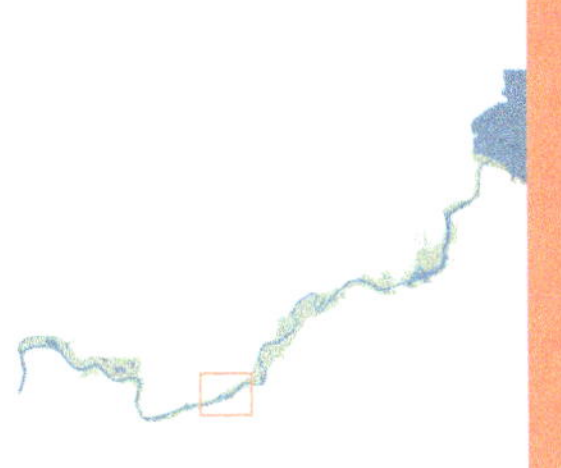

OVERVIEW

This stretch of river along the north bank has many well-worn trails. It is common to pass dog-walkers and runners, and even the occasional high school science class on this stretch of wild space. It is easy to find a spot that feels far from civilization just a half-mile from your car.

One unique feature found here is the long island in the middle of the river, starting in front of Rio Americano High School and ending around Estates Dr. The island splits the river so that the faster, deeper water flows along the south bank, leaving this stretch of river along the north bank shallow and protected.

In some spots, there are four or five parallel trails from which to choose: the levee path, a gravel trail, the paved bike path, and finally one or two different foot trails along the bluffs by the river.

GETTING THERE

From Hwy. 50, take Watt Ave. north. Turn right on American River Dr. Turn right onto either Estates Dr, Jacob Ln., or Ashton Dr. Park where any of these three streets dead ends, walk through the gate in the fence, up the stairs, and over the levee. No fee.

AMENITIES

Benches, signs

A RIVER SPOT AT ASHTON DRIVE

0.1 mile, Sun/partial shade, Swimming, Wading, Sand

Park at Ashton Dr. Head up and over the levee, down the concrete stairs, cross over the bike path (it can be busy — look both ways!), and make your way down to the river. You will find shady trees and a river bank perfect for a picnic.

B RIVER SPOT AMONG THE REEDS

0.25 mile, Sun/partial shade, Swimming, Wading, Sand

Park at either Ashton Dr or Jacob Ln. Just down-river from Rio Americano High School you'll see a grove of trees hugging the river. Follow the trail around this bend, stopping at any spot along the river to play. This is a great spot for boats and also for swimming. Find the rope swing hanging down from a huge oak tree.

Harrington Way
TO WILLIAM B. POND
HARRINGTON WAY RIVER ACCESS
P
Jacob Ln.
P
P
RIO AMERICANO HIGH SCHOOL
GRISTMILL RECREATION AREA
AMERICAN RIVER
C

BONUS ADVENTURE
Bring a blow-up raft and paddle out to one of the islands for a picnic!

SLOW WATER AND SANDY BOTTOM MAKE THIS AREA GREAT FOR SWIMMING

C RIVER SPOT TO THE PENINSULA

1.2 miles, Full sun, Kid, Picnics, Swimming, Wading, Clay/pebbles

Park at Jacob Ln. and walk through the gate, over the levee, and across the paved bike path to connect with the bluff trail. Walk downriver a half-mile until you see a trail branch off toward the river, under the trees, just in front of Rio Americano High School. Follow the 0.3-mile narrow foot path to the end of the peninsula. There is a trail along the south side of the island that will take you through the reeds and down to a sandy beach.

Access from Ashton Dr., visit the beaches among the reeds along the way (Adventure 7B)

Access from Harrington Way and follow the trail downriver that starts at the parking lot by the public bathroom. When you get to the white post where the trail forks, head right down the trail to cross the creek and then up to the bluff trail. Adds 1 mile.

D LOOP TO HARRINGTON RIVER ACCESS

3 miles, sun/partial shade, running, walking

This loop has something for every adventurer: wide dirt trails, river views, and a variety of sunny and shady spots. The fall colors are radiant along this stretch. Follow the bike path or the dirt trails to Harrington River Access and back, enjoying the trail that hugs the bluffs and winds underneath the tree canopy along the river's edge.

VARIATION:

Add two miles and continue through William B Pond until you reach the scenic overlook on the Harold Richey Memorial Bridge.

8

WILLIAM B POND RIVER ACCESS

5700 Arden Way, Carmichael, CA 95608

OVERVIEW

William B. Pond Recreation Area offers adventures of all kinds. It has large grassy areas, a splashy river spot, walking adventures that feel far off the beaten path, and a still pond. Across from the entrance is the Harold Richey Memorial Bridge. The bridge connects to River Bend Park on the south bank, allowing for long trail runs in either direction.

Directly after entering the park, you'll see the headquarters for the American River Parkway Foundation (ARPF) on your right. Here, you can purchase an Annual Parks Pass, as well ARPF t-shirts, hats, activity books, and stickers.

This area is named after the first Sacramento County Regional Parks Director, William B. Pond—not to be confused with Arden Pond, an old quarry from the mining days, separated from the river by a gravel dike.

GETTING THERE

From Hwy. 50, take the Watt Ave. exit north, right on Fair Oaks Blvd. Take a left on Arden Way all the way until it enters the parking area. Parking $7/day, or Parks Annual Pass.

ALTERNATIVE ACCESS POINTS

Harrington Way River Access
River Bend Park

AMENITIES

Bathrooms, picnic tables, water fountains, signs, benches.

A CLAY BANKS

0.1 mile, Sun/partial shade, Kids, Picnics, Swimming, Wading, Clay/pebbles

This is safe little swimming spot, away from the main current. When the river is low, it has a fast current over a very shallow wash which makes it great for toy boats, wading, and rock-hopping. There is also a swimming hole right in the center that bubbles like a cold jacuzzi tub. During a wet winter, the rapids here rage and surfers take turns on the standing waves.

Park close to the parking kiosk, walk over the lawn, across the bike path, and down an open gravel area to the river. Head a little upriver to find a slow, waist-high pool of sandy-bottom water for swimming. Head downriver where the trees cast shade and the river slows. On low-flow days, see if you can rock-hop all the way to the islands!

B BEACH DOWNRIVER

0.5 mile, Sun/partial shade, Kids, picnics, Swimming, Wading, Clay/pebbles

This beach spot is a little downstream from Clay Banks (above). The walk is a little longer, but there are fewer people and the river moves slowly here.

RIVER BEND PARK
Arden Way
THE AMERICAN RIVER PARKWAY FOUNDATION
American River Dr.
Harold Ritchie Memorial Bridge
AMERICAN RIVER
P
E
P
F
A
B
D
C
ARDEN POND

C SMALL HIKE TO THE WASH

2 miles, Sun, Kids, Picnics, Swimming, Wading, Rocky

Park at the middle parking lot by the paved path. This two-mile out-and-back journey will take you along an exposed trail past the pond and out to where the river bends. When the river is high, there is a creek crossing where the river flows into Arden Pond. The water is deeper and faster here, so while it's not the best spot for swimming, the rocky beach feels secluded, and you can set up a picnic and throw rocks. Keep your belongings light—this isn't the type of trail you want to travel while carrying a beach bag and a shade tent.

D ARDEN POND

0.1 mile, Sun, Kids, Picnics, Swimming, Wading, Clay/sandy bottom

Park at the final parking lot, and walk across the bike river trail and down to the water's edge. Paddle out to the islands—the warmer temperature of this pond makes it a great spot for swimming. Bring your blow-up kayak, or anything to float on, and cruise lazily around this shallow, warm pond. It is a great spot to bring your goggles and take some laps. Lather up in sunblock, lie back, and let your kiddos paddle you around in circles.

E LOOP UPRIVER (TO HAGAN PARK)

6 miles, Partial shade, Running, Walking

Grab one of the first parking spots close to the bridge as soon as you enter William B Pond. Follow the bike path over the bridge. On the other side of the bridge, take the first opportunity to head down to the left toward the grassy area and parking lot of River Bend Park. Cross the parking lot toward the river, up the berm to connect with the dirt trail. If you have ever floated the river, you'll recognize this area as the pull-out spot for rafters. Continue upriver along the dirt trail. The views of the trail from the bluff are beautiful—on a clear day, you can even spot the snow-capped Sierra Nevada range in the distance.

At the top of River Bend Park, take the trail to connect with the bike path for a few hundred feet and over the creek. Hug the trail until you get to Hagan Park. The trail from Hagan Park cuts right between the bike path and the river, past some of the river's most pristine, slow-moving waters near Ancil Hoffman. Choose a point to turn around and make your way back to the car. "Gilligan's Islands" here (picnic spot of adventure 12B) is one of my favorite turnaround spots to stretch, splash my head with water, and take in the honking geese.

VARIATIONS: *Park at River Bend at the top parking lot (see adventure 10D)*

Park at Hagan Park and run in reverse.

F LOOP DOWNRIVER (TO ASHTON DRIVE)

6 miles, Sun/partial shade, Running, Walking

This long, well-used trail is sunny and exposed—great for morning and winter runs. Start at William B Pond and run downriver along the bike path, past the pond to your left. At the first opportunity, take the dirt trails that head along the river. In some sections, there are several well-worn dirt paths to choose from. I recommend taking one on the run down, and the other on the run back. For a simpler experience, run the bike path down and back, past Rio Americano High School.

VARIATIONS: *Park at Harrington River Access*

Skip the parking fee and park off Ashton Dr. or Estates Dr. and run the opposite direction.

9

SARAH COURT RIVER ACCESS

5931 River Oak Way, Carmichael, CA 95608

THE SANDY-BOTTOMED INLET MAKES THIS A GREAT PLACE FOR SWIMMING.

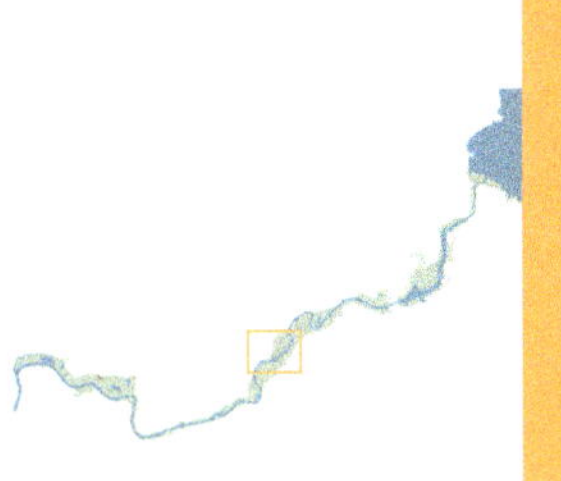

OVERVIEW

Sarah Court is nestled in an elite pocket neighborhood with one of the best sandy beaches along the river. Unlike other access points, this one does not connect with the extensive trails along the American River Parkway so it doesn't draw many crowds. The small parking lot has a gate that is closed in the summer months, but parking in the neighborhood and walking in is permitted.

GETTING THERE

From Hwy. 50, take Sunrise Blvd. exit north, left on Fair Oaks Blvd., left onto Oak Ave., right on Boyer Dr. which becomes Sarah Ct. There's a small shaded parking lot on the left hand side. No fee.

AMENITIES

None

IDEAL RIVER-FLOW:
Low to medium

SUN EXPOSURE:
Full sun

BEACH TYPE:
Clay, sand

TRAIL TYPE:
Dirt trail

ACTIVITIES:
Kids, picnics, swimming, wading

DOG-FRIENDLY:
Yes - on leash

PARKING:
No Fee

LOOK FOR:
California poppy
Blackberry
Great egret

A CLAY BANKS

0.1 mile, Sun, Kids, Picnics, Swimming, Wading, Clay

Walk down the wooden stairs from the parking lot and enjoy sitting on top of the clay banks or floating toy boats in the pools of water.

B SANDY POINT

0.25 mile, Sun, Kids, Picnics, Swimming, Wading, Sand

For a true bite-sized adventure, continue walking up the mesas and around the marsh. Cross over a little log bridge and up a sandy hill until you reach a spot with deep, fluffy sand perfect for digging or just throwing down a blanket and reading a book. The eddy makes a great sandy-bottomed swim spot.

WETLANDS NEAR THE RIVER

10

RIVER BEND PARK

2300 Rod Beaudry Dr., Sacramento, CA 95827

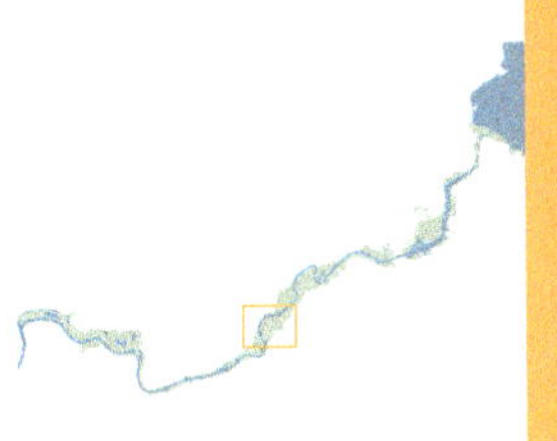

OVERVIEW

This vast, protected area is full of trails and remote beaches. It is also the take-out spot for American River Raft Rentals and can be quite busy during the warm months. Located between the American River Bike Trail and the river itself, the park is home to a web of interconnected trails and picnic spots crossing roughly four hundred acres of remote land.

GETTING THERE

From Hwy. 50, take the Bradshaw exit and turn right onto Folsom Blvd., then turn left on Rod Beaudry Dr.. Parking $7/day, or Parks Annual Pass.

ALTERNATIVE ACCESS POINTS

William B Pond
Hagan Community Park

AMENITIES

Bathrooms, picnic tables, water fountains, signs, benches.

IDEAL RIVER-FLOW:
Low to medium

SUN EXPOSURE:
Sun and shade

BEACH TYPE:
Rocky

TRAIL TYPE:
Dirt trail, bike path

ACTIVITIES:
Kids, picnics, swimming, wading

DOG-FRIENDLY:
Yes - on leash

PARKING:
$7

LOOK FOR:
Black-tailed deer
Elderberry tree
Swallow-tail butterfly

BONUS ADVENTURE

Grab a raft and spend a lazy day floating the river. Leave a car here, and shuttle up to Sunrise Blvd. If you rent from American River Raft Rentals, a complimentary shuttle will return you to your car.

A RIVER SPOT AT LOWER PARKING LOT

0.1 mile, Sun, Kids, Picnics, Swimming, Wading, Rocky

The large, rocky beach located at the end of Rod Beaudry Dr. is one of the easiest spots to reach. Park at the main parking lot and find a spot along the stretch extending down to the Harold Richey Bridge. The river is deep and relatively slow moving here, and this is where the rafters end their summer floats. In summer months, it can be busy.

B RIVER SPOT AT UPPER PARKING LOT

0.1 mile, Sun, Kids, Picnics, Swimming, Wading, Clay/rocky

Follow signs to the Upper Picnic Area and park at the dirt parking lot. Directly across the river from Sarah Court River Access is a great spot for wading, floating boats, and fishing. When the river is high, this beach fills with ankle-deep water.

C RIVER SPOT AT CORDOVA CREEK

1 mile, Sun, Kids, Picnics, Swimming, Wading, Hiking, Clay

For a slightly longer adventure with an excellent swimming hole, make your way up from the Upper Picnic Area along the trails around the bend where it opens up onto a wash. Just downriver from where Cordova Creek spills into the river, you'll find a branch of the river that is great for swimming.

D LOOP AROUND RIVER BEND PARK

3 miles, Partial shade, Running, Walking, Dirt trail, Access roads

Create a loop around River Bend Park, for a tour of exposed rocky park roads, shady bluffs, and meadow trails. From either parking lot, take the trail along the river's edge to Cordova Creek, then run back along the inland trail until it connects to the American River Bike Trail.

VARIATIONS: Park at William B. Pond adding 0.5 mile.

Extend this run another two miles by continuing past Cordova Creek and upriver to Hagan Park.

ANCIL HOFFMAN PARK
SARAH COURT
AMERICAN RIVER
B
A
C
TO HAGAN PARK
CORDOVA CREEK
P
P
P
D
Haroid Ritchie Memorial Bridge
Goethe Park Rd.
Rod Beudry Dr.
WILLIAM POND

11

ANCIL HOFFMAN

6700 Tarshes Dr., Carmichael, CA 95608

THERE IS EXCELLENT TREE CLIMBING AT ANCIL HOFFMAN

OVERVIEW

Ancil Hoffman Park is home to the Effie Yeaw Nature Center, which makes it an excellent destination for curious minds. Pop into the Visitor Center to see the exhibit hall of local wildlife taxidermy, pick up a birding book in the gift shop, or meet one of the resident animals, like Echo the owl. Check the calendar of events to attend a docent-led nature walk.

The 100-acre Nature Study Area does not allow bikes or dogs. Visitors can walk along the trails, read the signs, and see deer lazily grazing.

Although Effie Yeaw can steal the show, the rest of the 400-acre park has plenty to offer. It includes the Ancil Hoffman golf course, grassy picnic areas, sandy beaches, and a cross-country course trail looping the park.

GETTING THERE

From Hwy. 50, take Watt Ave. north. Turn right on Fair Oaks Blvd., right on Oak Ave., left on California Ave., and then right on Tarshes Dr. Parking $7/day, or Parks Annual Pass. Also available: Effie Yeaw Parking Pass.

AMENITIES

Effie Yeaw Nature Center, bathrooms, benches, signs, golf course.

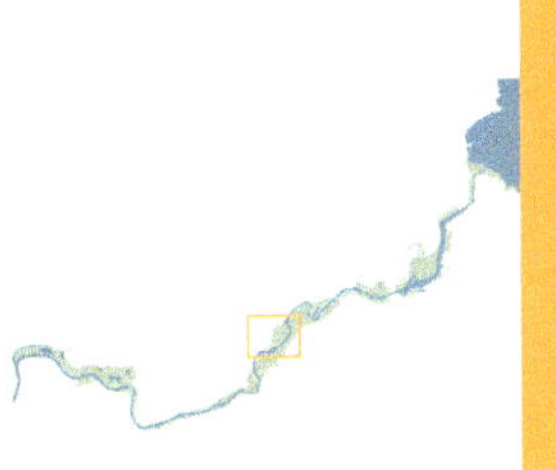

IDEAL RIVER-FLOW:
Any

SUN EXPOSURE:
Sun and shade

BEACH TYPE:
Rocky, sandy

TRAIL TYPE:
Dirt trails,
paved pathway

ACTIVITIES:
Kids, picnics,
swimming, wading,
running, walking

DOG-FRIENDLY:
Prohibited in the
Nature Study Area

PARKING:
$7

LOOK FOR:
Oak gall
Deer
Aorn woodpecker

A **EFFIE YEAW ROCKY WASH**

1 mile, Sun/partial shade, Kids, Picnics, Wading, Rocky

Park at the Nature Center, and follow the meandering trails toward the river. Skip rocks, roll up your pant legs, have a picnic, or watch the salmon spawning in the fall.

B **CLIMBING TREE/DINOSAUR NEST**

0.25 mile, Sun/partial shade, Kids, Picnics, Wading, Rocky

My kids never tire of climbing this cool tree. The dirt has eroded around the tree and left the root system entirely exposed. Imagine climbing on a root system like a spider web! There's a gigantic pile of rocks just upriver that we affectionately call the 'dinosaur nest.' It's great for perching in the center while munching on a granola bar.

C **BEACH SPOT WITH SMALL SHADY TREES**

0.1 mile, Sun/partial shade, Kids, Picnics, Wading, Sand

Bring your sand toys and beach blanket, and enjoy this section of slow-moving water. The river is shallow along the edge, but deepens quite a bit as you move out toward the middle. Park by the golf course—it's only about a five-minute walk to this excellent spot.

BONUS ADVENTURE

Bring an inflatable kayak and paddle across to the other side (below Hagan Park) and enjoy scrambling around on the clay mesas.

Palm Dr.
San Lorenzo Way
EFFIE YEAW NATURE CENTER
P
D
CARMICHAEL CREEK
E
NATURE STUDY AREA
A
P
P
Tarshes Dr.
P
B
ANCIL HOFFMAN GOLF COURSE
P
C
HAGAN COMMUNITY PARK
AMERICAN RIVER

D LOOP AROUND GOLF COURSE

3 miles, Sun/partial shade, Running, Walking, Dirt trails

Park in any lot to connect with this perimeter trail. The loop around the golf course includes some fun hills to add a little variety.

VARIATION: *Tack on a couple more miles by continuing along the trails in the Effie Yeaw Nature Area.*

E LOOP AROUND EFFIE YEAW NATURE AREA

2 miles, Shady, Running, Walking, Dirt trails

Park at the Effie Yeaw Nature Center lot. Choose your own adventure: bring your binoculars, and nibble on a snack on the benches set along the river and bluff trails.

HUMAN INTERFERENCE

Directly in front of the golf course is a water tower. This is one of the several sites along the Lower American River where channels have been dredged for the purpose of creating spawning habitat for the Chinook salmon, whose upriver habitat is inaccessible due to the Nimbus Dam.

EFFIE YEAW NATURE STUDY AREA

HAGAN COMMUNITY PARK

2197 Chase Dr., Rancho Cordova, CA 95670

SLOW, DEEP WATER RUNS PAST HAGAN PARK

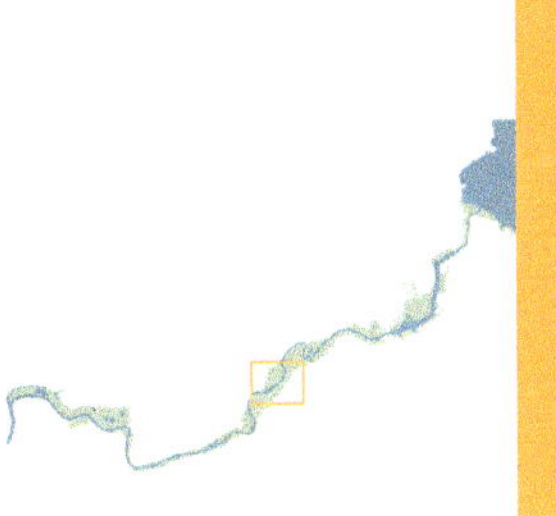

OVERVIEW

Hagan Park is more than just a river access point. There is a small steam train you can ride, a barn with resident petting zoo animals, an urban farm and market, a small fishing pond, play structures, a dog park, picnic tables, and baseball fields.

The trail that runs along the river below the bike path is scenic and feels remote (despite being easily accessible from such a well-established city park). Located directly across from the nature preserve at Ancil Hoffman, this stretch of slow-moving water is a great place to watch geese skid onto glassy water.

GETTING THERE

From Hwy. 50, take Mather Field Rd. exit, turn right on Folsom Blvd., left on Coloma Rd., left on Chase Dr.

AMENITIES

Restrooms, playground, picnic tables, dog park, fishing pond, soccer fields, tennis courts, steam train, petting zoo, Soil Born Farms.

IDEAL RIVER-FLOW:
Any

SUN EXPOSURE:
Sun and shade

BEACH TYPE:
Rocky, sandy

TRAIL TYPE:
Dirt trails, paved pathway

ACTIVITIES:
Kids, picnics, swimming, wading, running, walking

DOG-FRIENDLY:
Prohibited in the Nature Study Area

PARKING:
$5 Weekends only, May – September

LOOK FOR:
California wild grape
Kingfisher
Crayfish

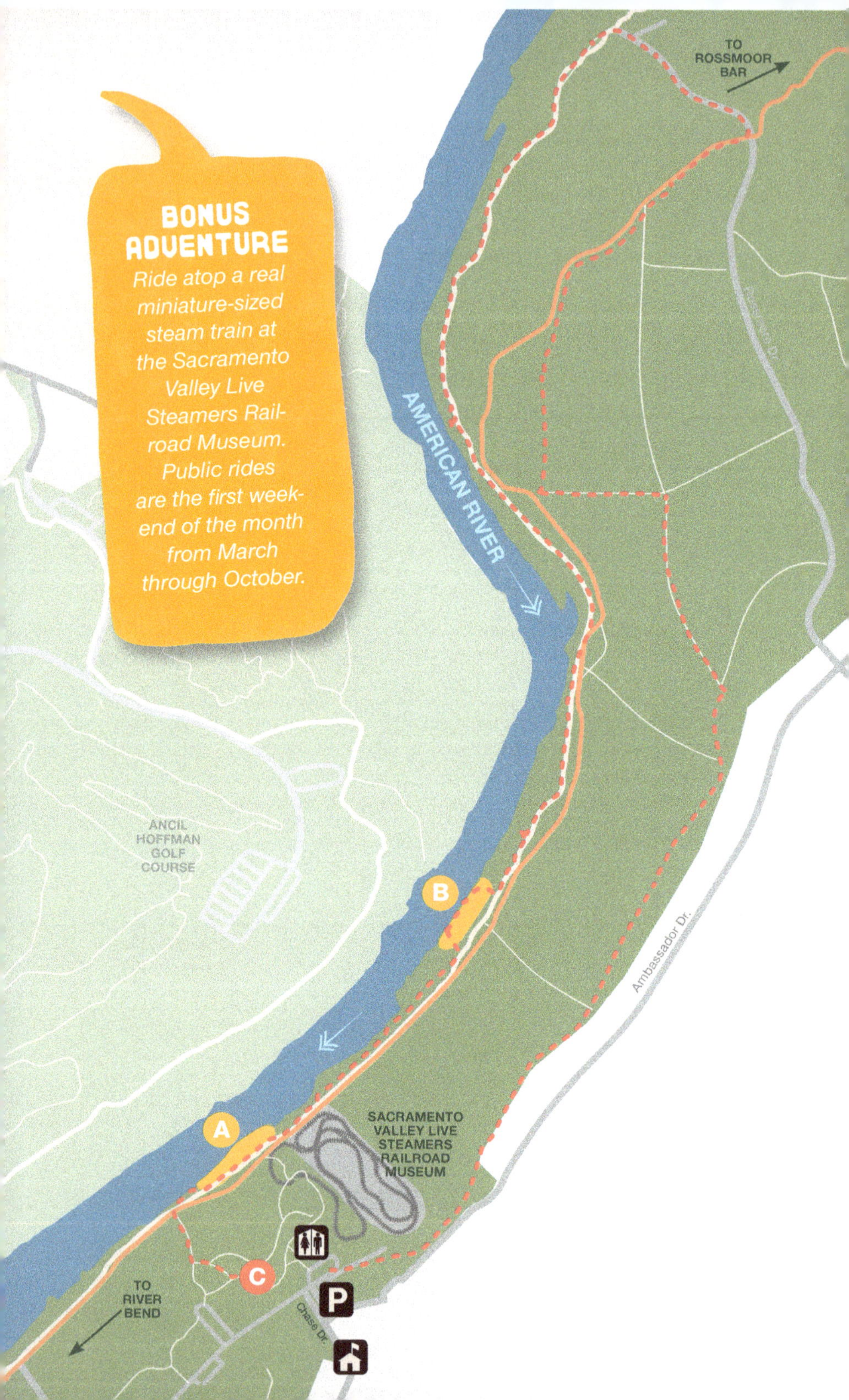

BONUS ADVENTURE
Ride atop a real miniature-sized steam train at the Sacramento Valley Live Steamers Railroad Museum. Public rides are the first weekend of the month from March through October.
TO ROSSMOOR BAR
AMERICAN RIVER
Rossmoor Dr.
Ambassador Dr.
ANCIL HOFFMAN GOLF COURSE
B
A
C
SACRAMENTO VALLEY LIVE STEAMERS RAILROAD MUSEUM
TO RIVER BEND
Chase Dr.
P

A WATER TOWER BANKS

0.1 mile, Sun/partial shade, Kids, Picnics, Wading, Rocky

There is a vast shelf of clay banks directly below Hagan Park, across from the water tower and the Ancil Hoffman Golf Course. When the water levels are high, the river is ankle deep; when the river is low, you can easily walk out like a tide pool and search for crawdads.

B GILLIGAN'S ISLANDS

1 mile, Full sun, Kids, Picnics, Wading, Clay

This is one of my favorite summer spots on the river, and an excellent stop during a float down-river. It is directly across from Ancil Hoffman's tree (11B). When the river is high, there is a submerged flat shelf, similar to a Baja shelf of a swimming pool. When the river is low, swimmers can stand atop the shelf and jump into deep water.

To access by land, park at Hagan Park. Walk toward the river, over the American River Bike Trail, and down to the dirt trail along the river's edge. Follow this about half a mile until you see it slope down to the clay banks.

HAGAN'S LARGE MEADOW IS GREEN AFTER THE RAIN

C LOOP UPRIVER TO ROSSMOOR BAR

3.5 miles, Sun/partial Shade, Running, Walking, Dirt trails, Fire road

Just below the bike path, this riverside trail feels remote and serene next to the slow-moving waters which reflect like a mirror on still mornings. The meadow trail is lush and full of wildflowers in the springtime. Keep your eyes peeled for coyotes in the wide open space.

Park by the playground and take the paved pathway toward the river, cross over the bike path to find the dirt trail that stretches along the river in both directions. Head upriver about 1.5 miles to Rossmoor Bar Access parking lot. From there, head back on the wide dirt path that runs below where the neighborhood meets the meadow. A little more exposed, there is a large meadow that separates the river from the neighborhoods along Ambassador Dr.

VARIATIONS: *Skip the meadow trail and stick to the river trail out-and-back.*

Downriver variation: Run downriver to River Bend Park. Take the wide gravel path that branches to the right until you cross the bridge over Cordova Creek. After crossing the bridge, immediately take the dirt trail to the right and follow the river trails out to the bluffs along River Bend Park. Also 3.5 miles. See 10D.

ROSSMOOR BAR RIVER ACCESS

1900 Rossmoor Dr., Rancho Cordova, CA 95670

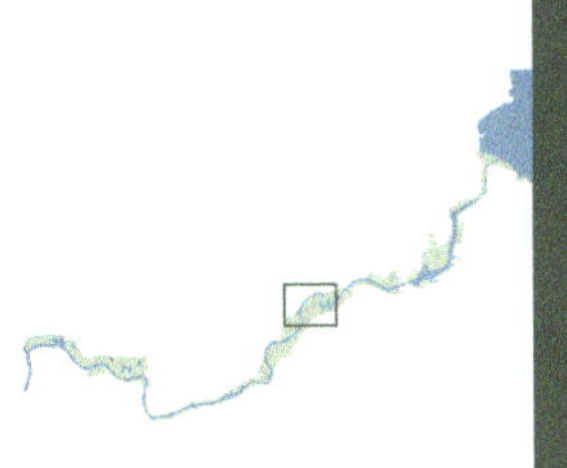

OVERVIEW

This secluded section along the south bank sits directly across from high cliffs, giving it the feel of a deep-water canyon. At the edge of the bar are the San Juan Rapids. These are the only Class II rapids along the Lower American River, and a great place to watch paddlers getting wet in the summer months. Some of the trails crossing the bar are made of smooth river stones the size of a fist, so tread carefully. This area was a gravel mining site so, just like other spots along the river, the piles of rock can make it seem a bit like you're exploring the moon.

GETTING THERE

From Hwy. 50, take Sunrise Blvd. north. Turn left on Coloma Rd., right on Rossmoor Dr. Parking $7/day, or Parks Annual Pass.

ALTERNATIVE ACCESS POINTS

El Manto River Access

AMENITIES

Bathrooms, boat launch.

HUMAN INTERFERENCE

In the early 1900s, this area was dredged heavily for gold, leaving behind huge mounds of gravel, called "gravel tailings" that can be up to 40 feet tall.

IDEAL RIVER-FLOW:
Any

SUN EXPOSURE:
Full sun

BEACH TYPE:
Sand and pebbles

TRAIL TYPE:
Dirt trails, fire road, rocky washes

ACTIVITIES:
Kids, picnics, swimming, wading, running, walking

DOG-FRIENDLY:
Yes

PARKING:
$7

LOOK FOR:
Fresh water clams
Golden field mustard
Rough-winged swallow

A **BEACH NEAR PARKING LOT**

0.1 mile, Full sun, Kids, Picnics, Wading, Swimming, Sand

Although it is only a hundred feet from the parking lot, this spot has all the necessary elements for a relaxing trip to the beach: sand and solitude. It is a great place to holler and hear the echo bounce off the canyon walls. After parking, walk towards the river. The beach just downriver from the boat launch is sandy and quiet.

B **BEACH UPRIVER**

0.5 mile, Full sun, Kids, Picnics, Wading, Swimming, Sand

After parking, take any of the parallel trails or fire roads upriver about a half-mile until you spot a large, sandy beach. This beach has plenty of room to explore, dig, and spread a picnic blanket. There is no shade, so bring your own or choose a time of day that is suitable.

C **LOOP AROUND ROSSMOOR BAR**

2.2 mile, Full sun, Runners, Walkers, All trail types

This loop follows the trails and maintenance roads that wind between the river and the American River Bike Trail. There are more trails to discover on the other side of the bike path and up to the neighborhoods, but it's pretty exposed.

After parking at the lot, head through the yellow posts to follow the trail out to the water and upriver. As the river bends, continue inland along the trail following it to a wide maintenance road. Turn left to the river and find yourself at the San Juan Rapids. Backtrack a few hundred yards and continue upriver along the wide road full of river rocks. You'll loop your way back when you reach the rock labyrinth below one of the parking lots at El Manto River Access. Head back on one of the inland trails towards your car.

VARIATIONS: *Continue along the river trail toward Sunrise Recreational Area, adds 2 miles.*

Continue downriver to Hagan Park, adds 1mile. Also 12C.

SAN JUAN RAPIDS
AMERICAN RIVER
A
B
C
P
P
P
BANNISTER PARK
EFFIE YEAW NATURE CENTER
Rossmoor Dr.
El Manto Dr.
Ambassador Dr.
Coloma Rd.
TO HAGAN COMMUNITY PARK

EL MANTO RIVER ACCESS

2000 El Manto Dr., Rancho Cordova

CLAY MESAS PROVIDE A SWEEPING VISTA

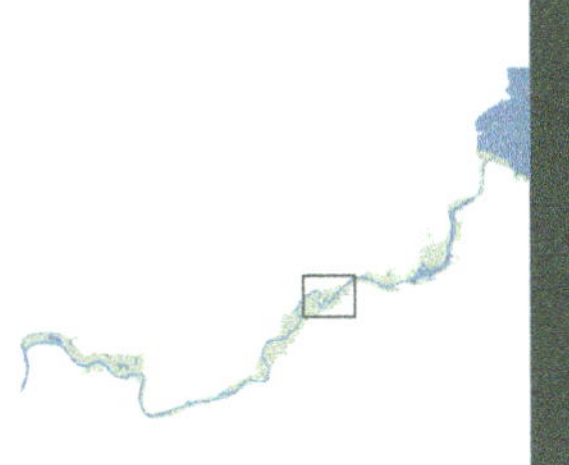

OVERVIEW

Here, where the river bends around Sacramento Bar, the water cuts deep past the clay banks. Spend a day perched on the banks, or lace up your shoes and take a long, remote trail in either direction. The terrain is variable along this section: the clay banks are red and vast, and downriver along Rossmoor Bar the trails are made of large, smooth river stones, while upriver along the bluffs the dirt trails provide sweeping vistas as far as Sunrise Blvd.

During the summer, this area can be filled with happy families barbecuing under shade tents watching floaters ready themselves for the San Juan Rapids just downstream.

GETTING THERE

From Hwy. 50, take to Sunrise Blvd. north. Turn left on Coloma Rd., right on El Manto Dr. Parking $7/day, or Parks Annual Pass.

ALTERNATIVE ACCESS POINTS

Ambassador Park
Lower Sunrise Recreational Area
Rosmoor Bar

AMENITIES

Bathrooms, benches

IDEAL RIVER-FLOW:
Any

SUN EXPOSURE:
Full sun

BEACH TYPE:
Clay

TRAIL TYPE:
Dirt trails,
bike river trail,
fire road

ACTIVITIES:
Kids, picnics,
swimming, wading,
running, walking

DOG-FRIENDLY:
Yes

PARKING:
$7

LOOK FOR:
Sapsucker
Blue oak tree
Redstem filaree

SAN
JUAN
RAPIDS
B
ROSSMOOR
BAR
AMERICAN RIVER
A
BANNISTER
PARK
C
P
P
AMBASSADOR
PARK
P
Ambassador Dr.
El Manto Dr.

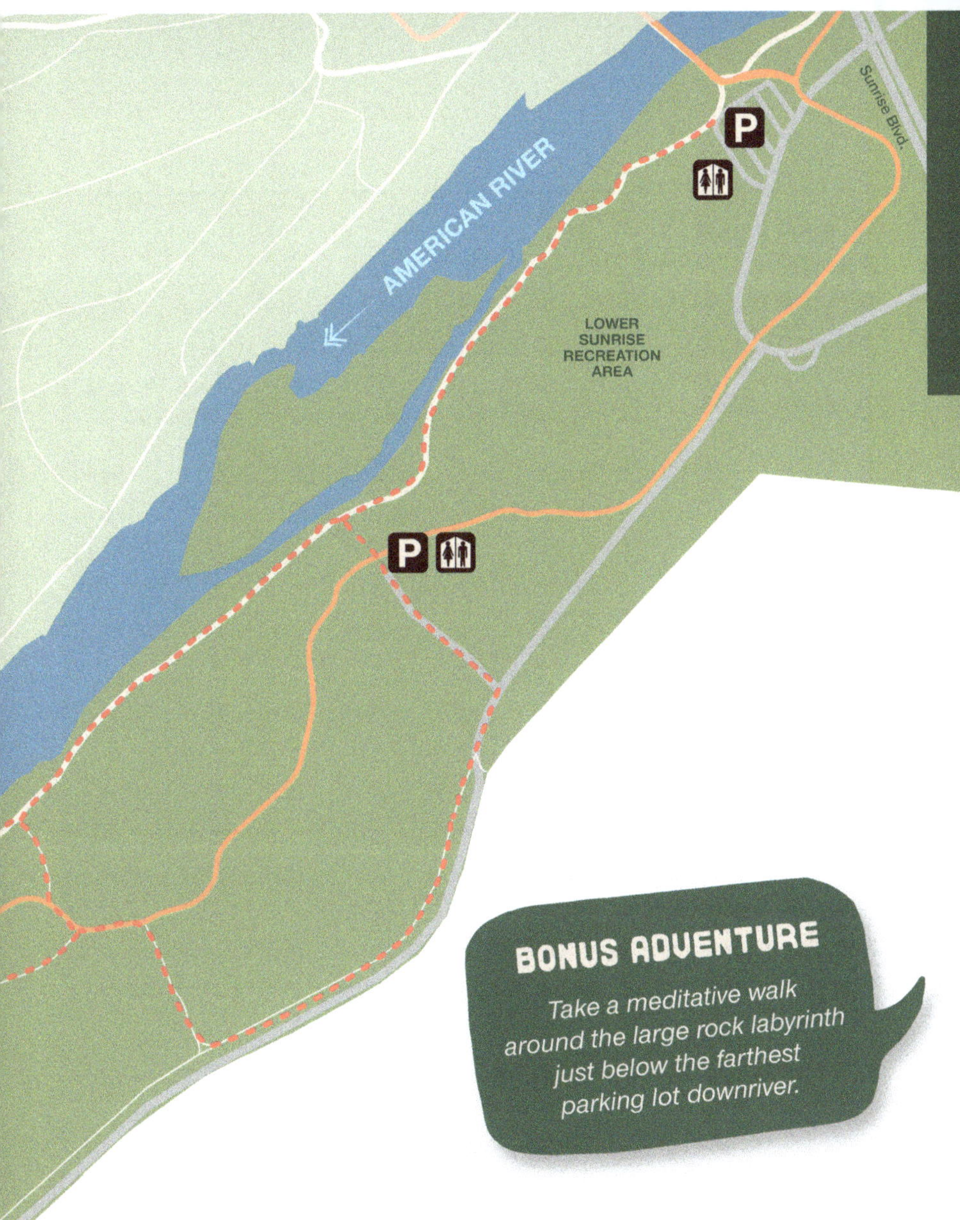

Ⓐ CLAY BANKS

0.5 mile, Full sun, Kids, Picnics, Wading, Clay

This spot can feel like exploring the surface of Mars with is wide red clay banks along the river. Downriver has an eddy great for swimming while the middle flats of the clay banks create a six-foot cliff excellent for jumping into deep pools.

Park in either the main parking lot or the farthest parking lot downriver.

B SAN JUAN RAPIDS DOWNRIVER

0.5 mile, Full sun, Kids, Picnics, Wading, Swimming, Rocks

Park at the parking lot farthest downriver and follow the wide gravel trail downriver. Stay to the right and follow the trail to the San Juan Rapids. Once you arrive on this secluded rocky beach, you'll be at the edge of what is called Rossmoor Bar (also accessible via Rossmoor River Access).

Pack a picnic and enjoy the feeling of being in a tropical canyon with a view of "swallow cliff" directly in front of you. On a weekend, you can spot rafters and paddlers braving the Class II rapids.

VARIATIONS: *Access via Rossmoor Dr. Also 13C.*

Make a loop by returning via the rocky maintenance road downriver from the San Juan Rapids

C LOOP TO LOWER SUNRISE

3.5 miles, Sun/partial shade, Running, Walking, Dirt trails

Start at the main parking lot and follow the trail about two miles upriver to the Jim Jones foot bridge. Return along the inland trail for variety until you cross the creek, making it a lollipop route.

VARIATIONS: *Park at the Lower Sunrise parking lot and run in reverse (also 15D).*

Park for free at the neighborhood parking lot at the intersection of Ambassador Dr. and Oaktown Way. This access point has a unique quarter-mile approach that lets visitors feel like they've hiked through a forest to arrive at the river.

VIEW UPRIVER TOWARD THE SUNRISE BRIDGE

15
SUNRISE RECREATIONAL AREA

11351 South Bridge St., Gold River, CA 95670

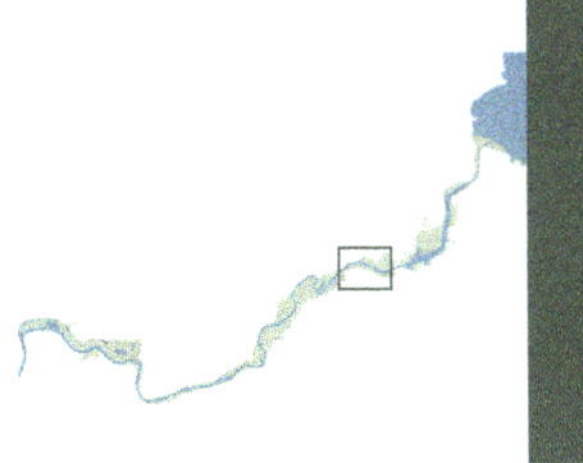

OVERVIEW

Sunrise Recreational Area is split into two sections: Upper and Lower Sunrise. Upper Sunrise extends upriver from Sunrise Blvd. to the Nimbus Dam, including a boat ramp underneath the iconic Fair Oaks Bridge. Lower Sunrise extends downriver from Sunrise Blvd. and is part of the larger section of river called Sacramento Bar (shared with Bannister Park across the river). It is connected by another foot bridge called the Jim Jones Bridge, named after the man who lobbied to keep the bridge even after the gravel mining trucks were retired in the 1970s.

In this park, there are several miles of wide, comfortable dirt trails heading in either direction, as well as endless beach spots, clay banks, and bluffs to perch upon and enjoy the views.

GETTING THERE

Take Hwy. 50 to the Sunrise Blvd. exit and head north to South Bridge St. The entrance to both Upper and Lower Sunrise is the same, taking you past a self-pay kiosk and into the large recreational area. Parking $7/day, or Parks Annual Pass.

ALTERNATIVE ACCESS POINTS

Nimbus Fish Hatchery

Fair Oaks Bridge

Gold River (private)

AMENITIES

Bathrooms, life jackets, picnic tables, boat launch, benches, signs.

IDEAL RIVER-FLOW:
Any

SUN EXPOSURE:
Sun and shade

BEACH TYPE:
Rocky

TRAIL TYPE:
Dirt trails,
ike river trail,
fire road

ACTIVITIES:
Kids, picnics,
swimming, wading,
running, walking

DOG-FRIENDLY:
Yes

PARKING:
$7

LOOK FOR:
Common snowberry
Bush monkey flower
Cliff swallows

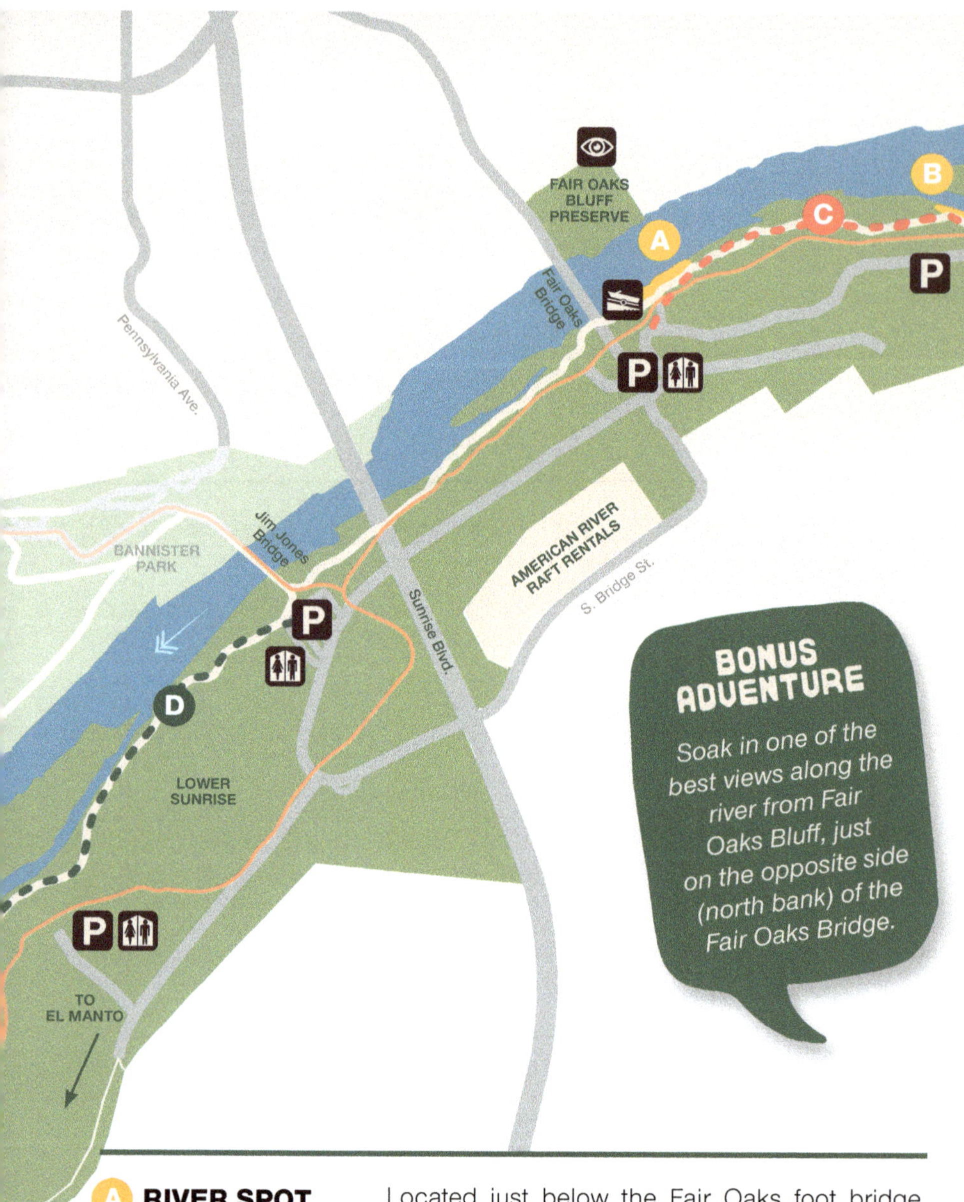

A RIVER SPOT BELOW BRIDGE

0.1 mile, Shade, Kids, Picnics, Wading, Dirt

Located just below the Fair Oaks foot bridge, this spot is great for watching boaters launch. Because the water is deep and slow-moving here, it is perfect for swimming, blowing up a raft and floating, or even swinging from one of the rope swings put up by locals. The beach itself is not wide, but there is plenty of shade to stay cool.

Park at the Upper Sunrise parking lot by the boat launch.

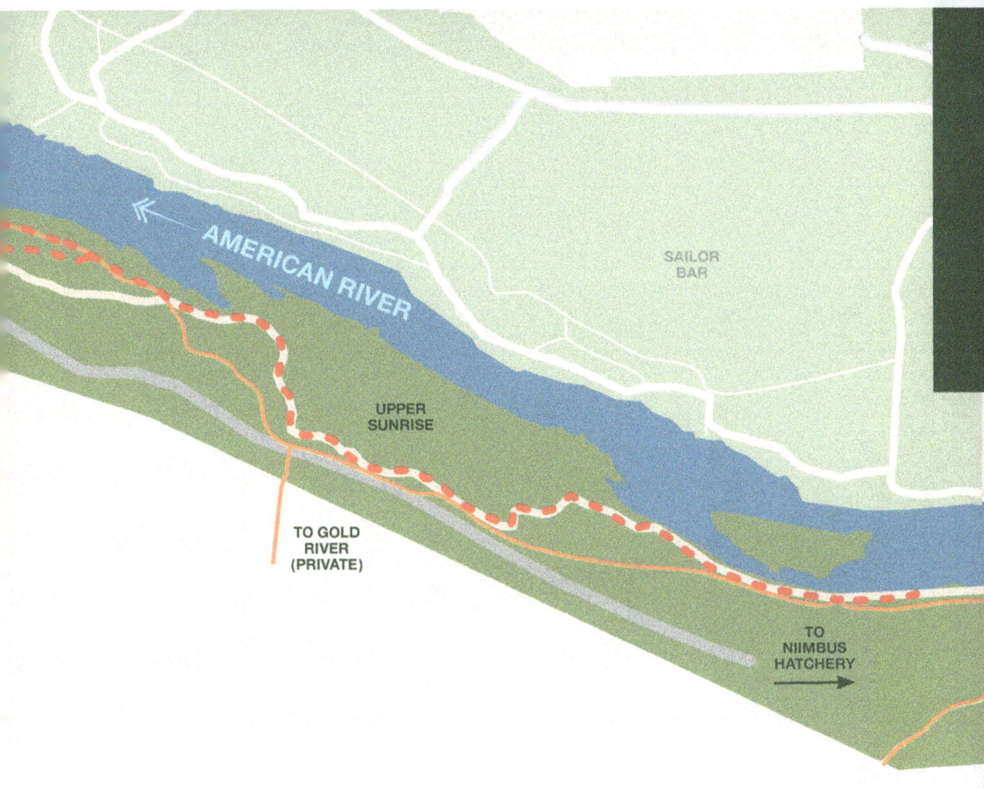

B SALMON SPOTTING

0.1 mile, Full sun, Kids, Picnics, Wading, Rocky

This is a great place to view the salmon, and because of this, it is also a popular spot for the opportunistic seagulls and vultures. There are dozens of fish here jumping, splashing, and spawning and you can gaze down from a bluff about 25 feet above.

Accessible by the American River bike path, as well as a simple drive. Enter Sunrise Recreational Area and drive upriver past the boat launch. Continue along the paved park road another half-mile and park along the wide dirt shoulder, once you can see the river on your left. There are benches and beaches from which to watch this incredible event.

WILDFLOWERS BLANKET THE UPPER SUNRISE TRAILS

C LOOP UPRIVER TO NIMBUS HATCHERY

3.5 mile, Partial sun and shade, Running, Walking

Park at the Fair Oaks Bridge parking lot and follow the trails upriver as they wind through the trees and vegetation along the river and out onto the bluffs. This stretch has some breaks in the cliffs that provide a slice of view out to Sailor Bar across the river. There are many little benches along the way with great views overlooking the river.

VARIATIONS:

Access through Gold River.

Park at Nimbus Hatchery and run in reverse.

D LOOP DOWNRIVER TO EL MANTO

4 miles, Partial shade, Running, Walking

This stretch of dirt trail is wide, flat, and ideal for walking or running side-by-side with a companion. It is a popular spot for birders. The canopy is high and lush, especially around the bend separating Sunrise and El Manto. Gaze down on the swift-moving water at the bend and all the way back upriver where you can spot Sunrise Blvd. in the distance.

VARIATIONS:

Turn around at Ambassador Park and return along the inland trail.

Start from El Manto (adventure 14C)

16

BANNISTER PARK

3820 Bannister Rd., Fair Oaks, CA 95628

RIVER SPOT AT THE SAN JUAN RAPIDS

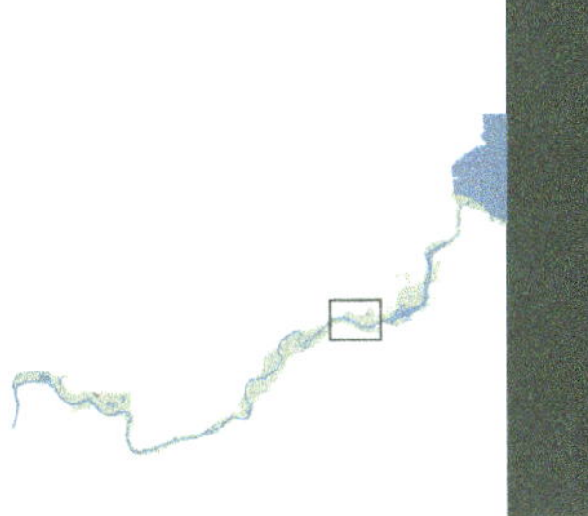

OVERVIEW

As part of the Fair Oaks Recreation and Parks District, Bannister Park is a great place to access Sacramento Bar and the vast area along the north bank of the river. The wide expanse of rocky wash features many trails crisscrossing this open space and, since the river bends dramatically around this near-peninsula, there is water on three sides. Stick to the widest trails, it's easy to get turned around. There is also a paved, shady bike path from the parking lot to the Jim Jones footbridge at Lower Sunrise.

GETTING THERE

From Hwy. 50, take Sunrise Blvd. north. Turn left on Fair Oaks Blvd., then left on Bannister Rd. Just before the road dead ends at the Waldorf School, turn left into a small parking lot after a soccer field with restrooms and an exercise area. No fee.

ALTERNATIVE ACCESS POINTS

Sacramento Bar Park at Pennsylvania Ave.
Lower Sunrise River Access at S. Bridge St.

AMENITIES

Bathrooms, water, benches, signs, exercise equipment.

IDEAL RIVER-FLOW:
Low

SUN EXPOSURE:
Full sun

BEACH TYPE:
Rocky, clay mesas

TRAIL TYPE:
Dirt trails,
rocky trails,
paved paths

ACTIVITIES:
Kids, picnics,
swimming, wading,
running, walking

DOG-FRIENDLY:
Yes

PARKING:
No fee

LOOK FOR:
Acorn Woodpecker
Milkweed

Fair Oaks Blvd.
Banister Road
BANNISTER PARK
SACRAMENTO WALDORF SCHOOL
SAN JUAN RAPIDS
A
C
AMERICAN RIVER
ROSSMOOR PARK
EL MANTO

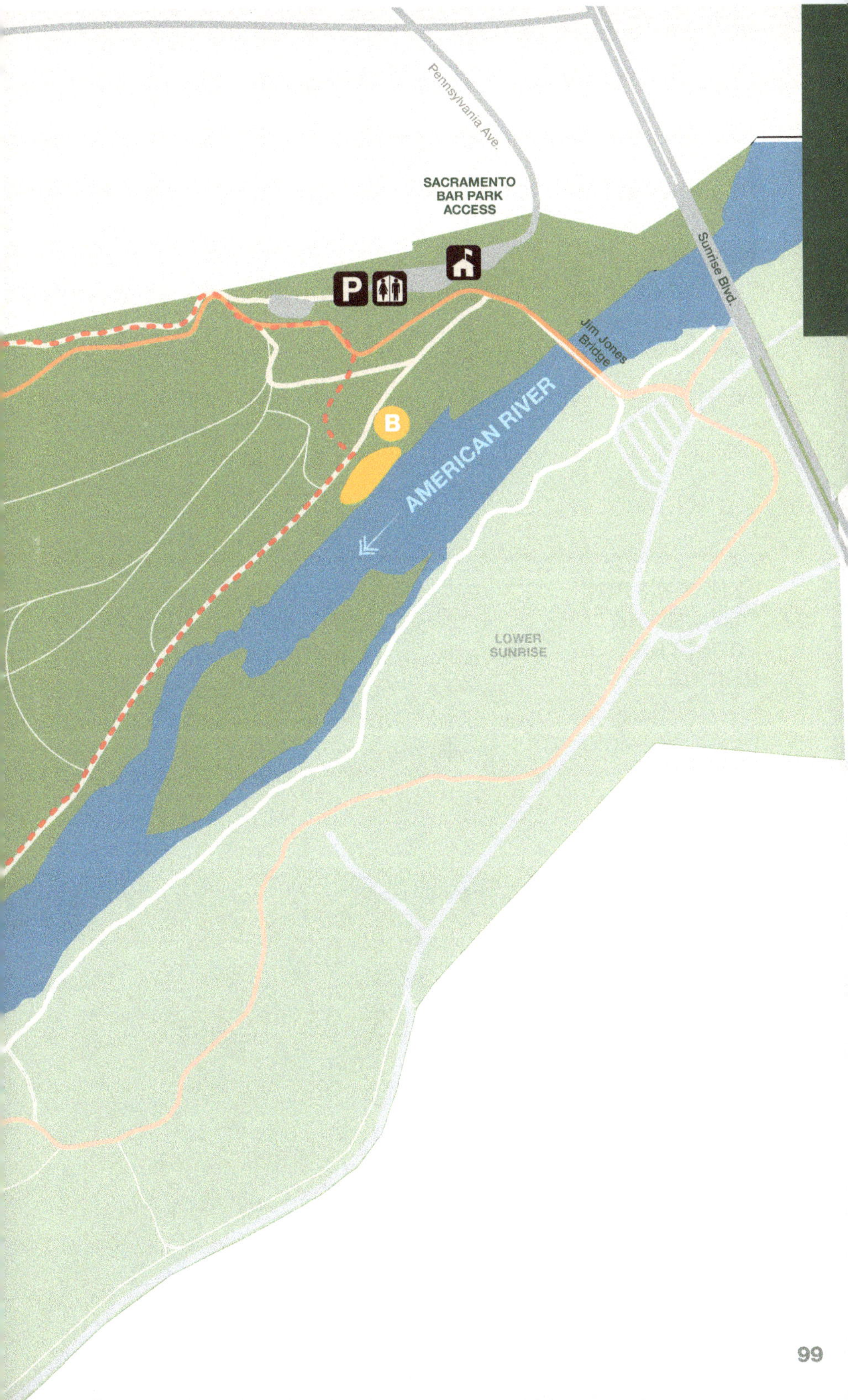

Pennsylvania Ave.
SACRAMENTO BAR PARK ACCESS
Sunrise Blvd.
Jim Jones Bridge
AMERICAN RIVER
B
LOWER SUNRISE
P

Ⓐ RIVER SPOT AT SAN JUAN RAPIDS

1 mile, Full sun, Kids, Picnics, Wading, Clay

This short adventure includes a hike with a few hills, and ends overlooking the San Juan Rapids, the only Class II rapid along the Lower American River. The clay banks here have been carved out by the fast-moving water and the result looks and feels like tide pools. Explorers can hop around safely while getting their feet wet. Stay away from the edge of the rapids, unless you are steady on your feet. Have a picnic where the water rushes by. When the river is high, the mesas are completely submerged.

Ⓑ RIVER SPOT DOWNRIVER FROM THE BRIDGE

1 mile, Full sun, Kids, Picnics, Wading, Rocky

This is a fun adventure that can easily be done with scooters, as the half-mile bike path from the parking lot to the river is paved. Alternatively, there is a dirt path that meanders roughly parallel to the paved pathway for a trail experience. The beach is rocky.

C LOOP AROUND BANNISTER PARK

3.0 miles, Sun/partial shade, Running, Walking, Dirt trails

This is a fun trail—partially under the shaded canopy of the trees, partially along the flat, wide maintenance roads, with some small trails along the bluff. There are several ways to make variations on this loop.

Start at the parking lot on Bannister Rd. and head down the paved trail toward the river. After crossing over the creek at the bottom of the hill, take the dirt trail to your left that parallels the paved walking/biking trail. When you reach the parking lot by the river (accessible via Pennsylvania Ave.), take a right along the maintenance road that heads downriver. Follow the wide path in a large loop around Sacramento Bar until it passes San Juan Rapids and returns to the paved bike path.

VARIATIONS: *Take any of the multiple maintenance roads that intersect Bannister Park.*

Find a little more adventure by heading off on the many foot trails along the water. The trails can be rocky in this area.

17

SAILOR BAR

8220 Olive Ave., Fair Oaks, CA 95628
4253 Illinois Ave., Fair Oaks, CA 96628

TREES SHADE THE RIVER BANKS NEAR OLIVE AVE.

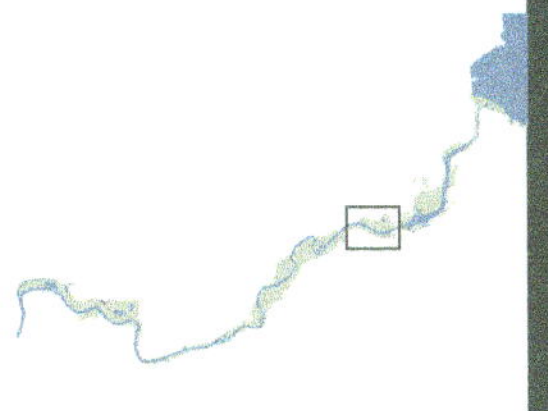

OVERVIEW

Accessible through the Fair Oaks neighborhood, Sailor Bar is an isolated stretch of the river that does not connect directly with the American River Bike Trail.

The western entrance, Olive Ave., has a parking lot in the middle of a rock quarry, and it feels a little like landing on an asteroid. Not to worry—although the parking lot is exposed, the trails along the river are lush and wooded. Take the trails through the yellow posts down to the river and you'll find some shady spots right along the water.

The eastern entrance, Illinois Ave., has a few gravel parking lots, including one by the boat launch. It's more exposed on this end of Sailor Bar, which makes it a sunny place ideal during the winter months and full of wildflowers in the spring. Besides being a popular boat launch, there are a variety of trails to explore, as well as a few shallow river spots great for wading.

GETTING THERE

Western entrance at Olive Ave.:

From Hwy. 50, take Sunrise Blvd. north. Turn right on Winding Way, right on Toyon Ave., right on Natoma Ave., and left on Olive Ave.

Eastern entrance at Illinois Ave:

From Hwy. 50, take Hazel Ave. north. Turn left on Winding Way, left on Illinois Ave. Drive all the way in, passing a parking kiosk.

AMENITIES

Pit toilets, Boat launch, Signs.

IDEAL RIVER-FLOW:
Any

SUN EXPOSURE:
Sun and shade

BEACH TYPE:
Rocky

TRAIL TYPE:
Dirt trails,
fire road, rocky

ACTIVITIES:
Kids, picnics,
swimming, wading,
running, walking

DOG-FRIENDLY:
Yes

PARKING:
$7

LOOK FOR:
Pond turtle
Beaver
Chinook salmon

A GRASSY BLUFF

0.1 mile, Shade, Kids, Picnics, Wading, Grass

At the Olive Ave. parking lot there is a trail that leads to a grassy bluff. In the spring, it is green and lush and the river glitters below. From atop the bluff, you can look out to the salmon channel at Upper Sunrise (Adventure 15B).

There is a trail that takes you down to a wide clay bank right along the rapids, nearly the height of the river. The water rushes around the bend, so keep the little ones close.

B BEACH SPOT

1 mile, Shade, Kids, Picnics, Wading, Dirt

After parking at Olive Ave., take the gravel road upriver and walk through the fifth pair of yellow posts. Alternatively, you can take the shady bluff trail until you reach the wide, rocky beach. This is a great place for a picnic or skipping rocks.

C SHALLOW BEACH

0.5 mile, Shade, Kids, Picnics, Wading, Rocky

Park at Illinois Ave. This beach is just long enough of a walk out to make it feel like an adventure for little legs. The river is shallow and moves rapidly in knee-deep water. This makes it fun to wade out—and a popular place to create little pools and rock formations with the smooth river stones. Bring your water shoes and plenty of sunblock as there is little to no shade.

D SALMON SPOTTING

0.2 mile, Sun, Kids, Picnics, Clay.

This protected canal has been excavated to make habitat for the salmon to spawn each fall. It is a great area for peering down over the impressive fish only a few feet away.

Enter Sailor Bar along the Illinois Ave entrance and drive all the way down toward the boat ramp. Park in either the ramp lot, or the large dirt lot just before for the boat ramp. Pass through the double yellow posts at the end of the lot to arrive at the canal.

E LOOP AROUND SAILOR BAR

3.5 miles, Shade and sun, Running, Walking

Park at either entrance. Depending on the amount of shade or sun exposure you seek, you can choose from a variety of trails that wind through Sailor Bar without exceeding four miles. The shady trail along the river, the gravel roads down the middle, and the wide, mostly shady gravel trail against the hill.

This loop adds a little topographical variety as you head up the steep, wide trail from the lower parking lot and up the ridge. There's a pond and nature area near the upper parking lot.

VARIATION: *Follow the trails through the 80-acre woodland area north of the pond.*

18
LAKE NATOMA

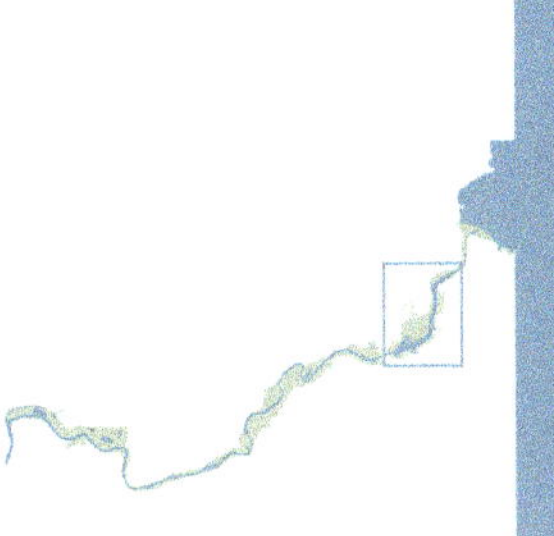

OVERVIEW

There are two lakes at the top of the Lower American River: Lake Natoma and Folsom Lake. Both are overseen by California State Parks, making the visitor experience more polished, regulated, and expensive than the Sacramento County experience of the other 17 chapters in this book. Between the city of Folsom and the California State Parks, there are a number of resources documenting the existing trails, so this chapter will be brief.

Lake Natoma sits above the Nimbus Dam at Hazel Ave. Bikers or runners can loop around the lake on the 11.5-mile paved trails, or you can make smaller adventures on foot by starting at any of the access points A–E and finding out-and-back adventures in either direction.

The following five adventures are in counter-clockwise direction, starting at the Nimbus Dam:

A. Nimbus Flat State Recreation Area

B. Willow Creek Recreation Area

C. Black Miners Bar State Recreation Area

D. Snipes-Pershing Ravine Trailhead

E. Mississippi Bar

LAKE NATOMA

- **A** NIMBUS FLAT STATE RECREATION AREA
- **B** WILLOW CREEK RECREATION AREA
- **C** BLACK MINERS BAR
  STATE RECREATION AREA
- **D** SNIPES-PERSHING RAVINE TRAILHEAD
- **E** MISSISSIPPI BAR

Greenback Ave.
BLACK MINER BAR
C
SNIPES PERSHING RAVINE
Rainbow Bridge
FOLSOM
B
P
Folsom Blvd.
50

VIEWS ARE GREAT FROM THE BLUFF

NIMBUS FLAT STATE RECREATION AREA

1901 Hazel Ave., Gold River, CA 95670

If you're looking for a place to stretch out a towel on the sand and swim in Lake Natoma, this is a great choice. There is a wide stretch of sand that can easily accommodate the many families who spend summer days relaxing lakeside. From this area, you can also watch boaters sailing the southern end of the lake from Sacramento State's Aquatic Center.

GETTING THERE

Take Hwy. 50 to Hazel Ave.

AMENITIES

Bathrooms, picnic benches, BBQ pits.

IDEAL RIVER-FLOW:
N/a

SUN EXPOSURE:
Any

BEACH TYPE:
Sand

TRAIL TYPE:
Dirt trails, bike path

ACTIVITIES:
Kids, picnics, swimming, wading, running, walking

DOG-FRIENDLY:
No

PARKING:
$10

LOOK FOR:
White-throated swift
Larkspur
Popcorn flower

FOR A BEACH DAY, simply park in the Nimbus Flat parking area right across from the large, sandy beach.

FOR A RUN OR HIKE, follow either the Jedediah Smith Memorial Trail or the lakeside American River Auxiliary Trail up the lake to Willow Creek Recreation Area (2.0 miles). For a longer challenge, continue to Folsom Bridge (4.4 miles).

FOR A PADDLING ADVENTURE, launch your craft on the sand and paddle up the lake to the Jedediah Memorial Bridge, exploring the inlet and waterway. Alternatively, you can paddle across the lake to Mississippi Bar where there are more inlets to poke around.

If you don't have a boat of your own, check out the Sacramento State Aquatic Center, which offers boat rentals, aquatic classes, and youth programs year-round. Sailboats, kayaks, SUPs) are among the many options for rentals.

CALM WATERS MAKE A GREAT SPOT FOR PADDLING

WILLOW CREEK
RECREATION AREA

13301 Folsom Blvd., Folsom 95630

This is a quieter spot than Nimbus flat, located where Willow Creek feeds into Lake Natoma. I don't recommend it as a beach access, since the shoreline here is either entirely vegetated, or quite rocky. It is great for picnics, boat launching, or accessing the bike path. The trails on this side of the lake have been well-maintained with a layer of decomposed granite stretching underneath the many Jeffrey pines.

GETTING THERE

From Hwy. 50, take Folsom Blvd. Turn left on Folsom Blvd., make a u-turn at Blue Ravine Rd., then turn right into Willow Creek Recreation Area.

AMENITIES

Bathrooms, picnic tables, informational signs, crushed DG trails.

FOR A TRAIL RUN OR HIKE follow the bike path up and across the bridge at Willow Creek where a gravel path branches off toward the water. This trail extends up to Folsom Bridge (3.0 miles), hugging the water's edge. Enjoy the are beautiful views of the glassy lake. Stop at any number of scenic picnic tables for a snack or as a turnaround point.

FOR A PADDLE LAUNCH your SUP or a kayak and paddle up the lake to Lake Natoma Island, or around the Willow Creek inlets.

FOR A FREE PARKING OPTION, try accessing this eastern stretch of Lake Natoma either from Parkshore Trailhead Parking Lot (1.0 miles from Willow Creek), or Young Wo Circle (2.0 miles from Willow Creek).

THE ICONIC RAINBOW BRIDGE

BLACK MINERS BAR
STATE RECREATION AREA

9800 Greenback Ln.,, Folsom, CA 95630

This access point is named after the newly-emancipated black gold miners who established the spot in the 1840s.

With a campground, BBQs, lifeguard towers, and flushing toilets, this spot is well-established with all the amenities of a state park facility. There are several spots from which to access Lake Natoma.

GETTING THERE

From Hwy. 50, take Folsom Blvd. Turn left on Folsom Blvd., right onto Greenback Ln, then left on Park Rd. Once through the kiosk, follow the park road to the right to the end and park by the bathrooms and lifeguard towers.

AMENITIES

Bathroom, campground, picnic tables, lifeguard towers, shade structures, boat launch.

IDEAL RIVER-FLOW:
N/a

SUN EXPOSURE:
Sun or partial shade

BEACH TYPE:
Sand

TRAIL TYPE:
Dirt trails, bike path

ACTIVITIES:
Kids, picnics, swimming, wading, running, walking

DOG-FRIENDLY:
Not in swim area

PARKING:
$10

LOOK FOR:
Barn swallow
Mountain lion
California poppy

FOR A PADDLING ADVENTURE, bring a kayak or a SUP and launch at the boat ramp, wind your way up to the tippy top of Lake Natoma, under Rainbow Bridge and past the giant boulders submerged along the way. Depending on the flow released by the Folsom Dam, there will be a current to paddle against on the way there, which makes it great for floating with ease back to the launch. Wondering why the water is so chilly here? The water flowing down from the Folsom Dam is that cold water held at the bottom of the lake!

FOR A BEACH EXPERIENCE, drive toward the far western edge where the lifeguard tower looks over a small beach. There are picnic tables under shade structures—great for a day of swimming and relaxing by the water.

FOR A SMALL WALK AND SOME ROCK JUMPING, drive to the far eastern edge of Black Miners Bar and follow the trail out to the water. There are huge rocks jutting out of the deep waters, making it a fun place for confident swimmers.

BRIDGE OVER DEEP RAVINE

SNIPES-PERSHING RAVINE TRAILHEAD

5600 Snipes Blvd., Orangevale, CA 95662

This is a unique trail in the region. It begins at the top of a ravine, winds down through a lush forest, and crosses over large and beautiful bridges until reaching Lake Natoma. Just at the bottom, there is a pond with lilies and snapping turtles sunning themselves on the logs. Cross over the bike path (carefully!) and the lake edge is right there. There isn't much beach, but there is enough to perch, put out a blanket, and eat a sandwich before climbing back to the car.

GETTING THERE

From Hwy. 50, take Hazel Ave. north. Turn right on Sunset Ave., left on Main Ave., right on Pershing Ave., right on Snipes Blvd. and park on the road where it meets Twin Lakes Ave.

AMENITIES

None

IDEAL RIVER-FLOW:
N/a

SUN EXPOSURE:
Shade or partial shade

BEACH TYPE:
Rocky

TRAIL TYPE:
Dirt trails, bike path

ACTIVITIES:
Kids, picnics, swimming, wading, running, walking

DOG-FRIENDLY:
Yes

PARKING:
No fee

LOOK FOR:
Blue oak tree
Purple needlegrass
California fuschia

MIDDLERIDGE TRAIL

MISSISSIPPI BAR

5200 Main Ave, Fair Oaks, CA 95628

There are a few neighborhood entrances to the Mississippi Bar network of trails. Some of the loops off of this access point are sometimes dirt, occasionally meeting up with the bike river trail. The loop on the map is a suggested route, but there are many other trails to discover from this access point.

Park where Sunset Ave. meets Main Ave., along the wide dirt shoulder. Behind the parking area is the trailhead for Middleridge Trail and Shady Trail, two parallel trails that take you about 1 mile down to Lake Natoma. Middleridge Trail stays along the grassy, exposed ridge, and provides stunning views of the lake below. Shady Trail cuts along the canyon under the shade of the oak trees.

At the bottom of either trail, take a left onto the paved bike path. After the bridge, veer right onto the wide gravel road and follow one of the trails closest to the lake around the entire bend until it meets with the bike path. Cross up over the bike path and return along the shady trails. About 5.5 miles.

GETTING THERE

From Hwy. 50, take Hazel Ave. north, then right on Sunset Ave. Park where Sunset Ave. and Main Ave. cross, there will be a wide dirt shoulder along the road along which to park. No fee.

AMENITIES

None

BEST ADVENTURES

BEST TRAILS: Guy West Bridge Loop, River Bend Park, Ancil Hoffman, Hagan Community Park, Rossmoor Bar, Bannister Park, Sailor Bar, Mississippi Bar

BEST SAND: Paradise Beach, Sarah Court, Ancil Hoffman

FREE PARKING: Sutter's Landing, Paradise Beach, Guy West Bridge, Waterton Way, Ashton Drive and Jacob Lane, Sarah Court, Bannister Park, Snipes-Pershing Ravine Trailhead

BEST SWIMMING: El Manto River Access, Paradise Beach, William B Pond, Beal's Point, Black Miners Bar

BEST SECLUDED ADVENTURES UNDER 1 MILE: Peninsula at Jacob Lane, William B Pond Small Hike to the Wash, Sarah Court, San Juan Rapids, Snipes-Pershing

WELL-WORN PATHS: Guy West Bridge, Estates Dr. to Jacob Ln, William B Pond, Hagan Park. Lower Sunrise

BEST BRIDGES: Fair Oaks (Sunrise Recreational Area), Harold Richey (William B Pond + River Bend), Rainbow Bridge(Black Miners Bar), Snipes-Pershing

BEST TREE CLIMBING: Ancil Hoffman, Sarah Court, William B Pond, Ashton Drive, Gristmill Recreation Area

BEST VIEWS: Jacob Lane, El Manto River Access, Fair Oaks Bluff, Sailor Bar at Olive Ave, Middleridge Trail at Mississippi Bar

BEST SALMON SPOTTING: Effie Yeaw, Upper Sunrise, Sailor Bar, Nimbus Hatchery

MILDLY RECOMMENDED:
SALMON
SPOTTING

CHINOOK SALMON

Every fall, the Chinook salmon make their impressive return home from the open ocean, back to their exact place of birth along the Lower American River. They typically spend four years out in the open ocean, traveling as far as Alaska, before their last and heroic spawning before they promptly die. Their nutrients upriver feed into the ecosystem, enriching the soil and the diet of the surrounding wildlife. While spawning, they thrash about in water, competing for space to spawn. Their powerful bodies can skid along the surface of shallow waters against impossibly strong currents. The water looks like a boiling soup of salmon fins. If you haven't seen it — you absolutely must check it out.

One of the reasons the river is federally-designated as a "wild and scenic river" is because it is a vital habitat for these endangered fish (in addition to the Steelhead Trout). Because of their invaluable impact on the environment, and the demise of their population due to dams and other human interference, there has been significant efforts to rebuild their spawning habitat in the last few years and the results have been immediate.

Wild salmon nest their eggs in riffles, or stretches of river where the water runs fast along shallow gravel. Recently, the Sacramento Water Forum has dredged several channels away from the main flow of the river. These channels have been carefully groomed for gravel that is just the right size for the salmon to create their redds (nests) and lay their eggs.

Here are four mildly recommended spots to view them:

EFFIE YEAW (11A) It is no surprise that the Nature Study Area of the Effie Yeaw Nature Center has a protected stretch of river dedicated to spawning salmon. This adventure requires a short walk, maybe half-mile.

From the visitor's center, follow the "Main Trail" out to the rocky beach. You'll find a quiet inlet, which serves as a sort of nursery where the new baby fish (called "fry") can grow up a bit before heading out to the ocean. On the far side of the inlet, you'll see the riffles where the salmon are spawning.

UPPER SUNRISE (15B)

This is a great place to view the salmon, and because of this, it is also a popular spot for the opportunistic seagulls and vultures. There are dozens of fish here jumping, splashing, and spawning and you can gaze down from a bluff about 25 feet above.

Previously, I'd named the island just above the Fair Oaks Bridge "Pirate Island" because it made a great place to wade over for a beach day. But that was before it was dredged out and became one of the best spots along the river to watch the salmon. Please don't wade across the channel — salmon redds (nests) are full of eggs and you might disrupt them!

Accessible by the American River bike path, as well as a simple drive. Enter Sunrise Recreational Area and drive upriver past the boat launch. Continue along the paved park road another half-mile and park along the wide dirt shoulder, once you can see the river on your left. There are benches and beaches from which to watch this incredible event.

SAILOR BAR (17D)

Sailor Bar is at the very top of the river, and the final option for wild salmon to spawn naturally before they run against the Nimbus Dam and need to take the fish ladder up to the Nimbus Fish Hatchery for their final act. The area is great for peering down over the fish as they nest and compete for the chance to fertilize.

Enter Sailor Bar along the Illinois Ave entrance and drive all the way down toward the boat ramp. Park in either the ramp lot, or the large dirt lot just before for the boat ramp. The channel is located just upriver from the boat ramp, and you can enter it from the far end of the dirt parking lot, or from the boat ramp lot - enter the double yellow posts.

NIMBUS FISH HATCHERY

While it might seem obvious to head to the Nimbus Fish Hatchery to see the salmon, heading down to where the fish ladder meets the water is a remarkable sight. The 40-pound fish leap several feet out of the water against the gates of the ladder, waiting for their turn to procreate at their exact place of birth — the hatchery.

After the dam was erected in the 1950s, the hatchery was created as a place for the critically endangered salmon and steelhead trout to spawn. It is one of only two fish hatcheries in Northern California. Between November and February, visitors can observe a spectacular natural phenomenon—fish making the incredible journey back from Alaska to their native hatching grounds. Year-round, visitors can feed the small fry who populate the hatcheries' raceways as well as learn about their life-cycle in the visitors center. Open daily 8am-3pm.

Located just below the Nimbus Dam at Hazel Ave. Turn off of Gold Country Blvd to Nimbus Fish Hatchery and walk the bike path (careful of the bikes zooming past!) under Hazel Ave bridge and down to the water. About 0.25 mile.

RESOURCES

PARK MANAGEMENT AGENCIES

Effie Yeaw Nature Center
(916) 876-4918
www.sacnaturecenter.net

Folsom Lakes State Recreation Area
(916) 988-0205
www.parks.ca.gov/?page_id=500

Sacramento City Parks and Recreation
(916) 808-5200
www.cityofsacramento.org/parksandrec/parks

Sacramento County Regional Parks
(916) 875-6961
https://regionalparks.saccounty.gov/Pages/default.aspx

RECREATION AND EDUCATION

American River Raft Rentals
www.raftrentals.com

Effie Yeaw Nature Center
www.sacnaturecenter.net

Hagan Community Barn
crpd.com/parks/hagan-community-barn

Nimbus Fish Hatchery
wildlife.ca.gov/Fishing/Hatcheries/Nimbus

River Rat Raft and Bike
river-rat.com

Soil Born Farms
soilborn.org

CONSERVATION AGENCIES

American River Conservancy
www.arconservancy.org

American River Parkway Foundation
arpf.org

CONSERVATION AGENCIES (CONT.)

American River Trees
www.americanrivertrees.org

Bushy Lake Restoration Project
www.bushylake.com

California Data Exchange Center (CDEC)
cdec.water.ca.gov

Effie Yeaw Nature Center
www.sacnaturecenter.net

Friends of Lakes Folsom and Natoma
folfan.org

Friends of the River
www.friendsoftheriver.org

Leave No Trace Center for Outdoor Ethics
www.lnt.org

Preserve the American River
www.preservetheamericanriver.org

Sacramento Audubon Society
www.sacramentoaudubon.org

Sacramento Water Forum
www.waterforum.org

Sacramento Valley Conservancy
www.sacramentovalleyconservancy.org

Save the American River Association
www.sarariverwatch.org

BOOKS

Donnelly, R. (2011). Biking and Hiking the American River Parkway. American River Natural History Association (ARNHA).

Hayes, P.J. (2013) The Outdoor World of the Sacramento Region. American River Natural History Association (ARNHA).

Hayes, P.J. (1977 or 2005 revised) The Lower American River Prehistory to Parkway. American River Natural History Association (ARNHA).

ACKNOWLEDGEMENTS:

Writing a book has been a project larger and more involved than I had ever imagined, and I am so thankful for the encouragement, advice, and collaboration of the many smart and adventurous friends and family members who believed in this project.

I would not have even considered writing the book had it not been for Sabrina Nishijima, author of *1,001 Things to Do in Sacramento with Kids* and owner of the East Village Bookshop who has been my guide and mentor for self-publishing from the moment I met her in the bookshop and blurted out my idea for this book. Her belief in me as an author has helped me see it myself.

A Mom is only as strong and innovative as her community, and I am lucky to have so many women in my life who have built a very successful passion project of their own and are reaching down the ladder to give me a hand. To Erin Ridley for being my first proof-reader and mentoring me through the process of creating a brand and a website from scratch. To Katie Dickson, whose local knowledge of Sacramento and the American River of the 90s has created invaluable background context for this book – sharing the river with you in the present tense has brought me real-time joy and motivation to keep going. To Laura Jensen, for being the first to chuckle at the title concept Mildly Scenic, and for infusing your love of travel, hiking, books, conservation and clever words into loving advice and counsel. To Jenn Eckerle who might have been the first person to tell me I should write a book. To Jillian Stefanki who can bundle my rambling excitement and weave it into a communications plan. To Sarah Rodriguez, local business owner and dear friend who showed me how to take a dream and make it reality. To Taren Redwine who taught me to use social media and sprinkled nuggets of wisdom during every bang trim over the past year. To Vanessa Gade for a wealth of creative and practical business advice – I'm lucky to have you in my corner.

So much of a guidebook is communication through the visual experience, which I could not have done without the incredible work of Greg Traverso. Not only did you manifest the brilliant logo, but you shared a vision for the grassroots movement that Mildly Scenic can (and will!) be. Your lens on the big-picture and on creating community through art has colored and shaped my book and I am so grateful to have your collaboration.

To Jen Wonnacott for introducing me to Greg Traverso in the first place. To Dierdre Wolonick for taking the maps on their first test runs and providing invaluable feedback. To the women in my Book Club who have kept my nose in a book and my mind enriched for nearly a decade. To the many more who have listened to me chat incessantly about the river and this book – thank you. This book was made better after my conversations with each of you.

To my editor W. Ezekiel Goggin, for your upbeat and thorough review of my manuscript and giving me confidence in the words I've written.

To the professors at Sac State, who lent their time and students to Mildly Scenic. From the Geography Department, Associate Professor Anna Klimaszewski-Patterson took the puzzle of building the trail maps from scratch and made a semester project out of it. I am so thankful for the hours of work that both she and her Fall 2023 students poured into these maps. From the Department of Design, Assistant Professor of Design Studies Marcy Wacker saw my plea for better PR for the river and mobilized her Spring 2024 students to design a solution.

To the river, my entire existence in Sacramento is intertwined with my love for you. You give me a place to be still, to process big things, to discover and explore, to access the traveler and teacher within me, and to foster the nature love within my children.

And of course, to all those before me who have enjoyed and protected the Lower American River long before I ever came along: American River Parkway Foundation (ARPF), Save the American River (SARA), Effie Yeaw and those at the Nature Center, and all of the photographers, dog-walkers, fisherman, birders, bikers and families I have met along the American River. Together we enjoy and protect this precious and wild river.

Writing this book took time. Time to explore the trails, and then time to write it all down. Neither of these would have been possible without our kids' teachers who make it possible for me to run the trails and write the book while they are in school.

To my parents, Lee and Doug Shult, and my sister Jessica and her husband Brian Huppi. You have fostered the entrepreneurial nature of this guidebook and gamely joined for any river adventure I have planned on your visits to Sacramento.

To my husband, Andy, who planted the seed for us to explore the river whilst the schools were closed during the pandemic, who gravel bikes the entire 50 miles of this book in one afternoon before dinner and is my go-to person when nerding out on the river.

Lastly, to my kids – without your boundless energy and desire to manipulate the environment around you I would have never explored the river trails so thoroughly. Each adventure in this book we did together, and so it is full of memories of turkey cheese sandwiches, sunscreen, and dirt galore.

ABOUT THE AUTHOR:
ASHLEY SHULT LANGDON

Raised in a family of travelers and teachers, Ashley had the great fortune of inheriting the thirst for exploring the unknown. Apart from a childhood in the Bay Area, she spent a couple of high school years in Malaysia, a couple of college years in Costa Rica, and a lot of her twenties leading trips to remote areas overseas. She studied Ecology, Behavior, and Evolution at UC San Diego but followed her hobby of travel and trip leading until it accidentally became a 20-year career. Now, she's gone ahead and taken another hobby and turned it into her first book.

Having seen some really scenic wild places around the world, she has found a special appreciation for the mildly scenic daily adventure: the kind of place that delivers the thrill of the natural environment without the hours of travel and vacation time. As a trail runner and a Mom of two energetic kids, the Lower American River has provided countless bite-sized adventures close to her home that she shares with her ruggedly handsome husband in Sacramento, California.

The river will continue to change and I invite you to share your discoveries and reach out with your questions in any of the following formats:

Email: hello@mildlyscenic.com
Instagram: @mildly_scenic
www.mildlyscenic.com

ABOUT THE DESIGNER:
GREG TRAVERSO

Greg Traverso is an artist, designer and creative director born and raised in Northern California. He specializes in developing creative and unique solutions to complex projects for a wide range of clients. He currently resides in Las Vegas, NV.

To connect with Greg and see more of his work:
Instagram: @greg_traverso
www.gregtraverso.com